Balestier Press
Centurion House, London TW18 4AX
www.balestier.com

The Bushmen (San) of Africa:
More than 40,000 Years of Learning
Copyright © Alan Barnard

First published by Balestier Press in 2022

A CIP catalogue record for this book
is available from the British Library

ISBN 978-1-7398937-2-9

All rights reserved. No part of this publication may be reproduced, stored in a retrieval system or transmitted in any form or by any means, electronic, mechanical, without the prior written permission of the publisher of this book.

Design, pagination and production by John at mapperou@gmail.com

Photo credits: Cover: Man with dancing rattles
Rock painting in Twyfelfontein, Namibia by Schnobby.
CC BY-SA 3.0, commons.wikimedia.org/w/index.php?curid=19141429

All illustrations are by Alan Barnard except photo 4 which is from Wikipedia, photo 15 by Julie Grant and photo 18 by Graham Hamilton. Figure 6 is from Wikipedia.

****

THE BUSHMEN (SAN) OF AFRICA

More than 40,000 Years of Learning

ALAN BARNARD

*Emeritus Professor of the Anthropology of Southern Africa
University of Edinburgh*

|

Balestier Press

www.balestier.com

Singapore | London

About the author

ALAN BARNARD is Emeritus Professor of the Anthropology of Southern Africa at the University of Edinburgh. He lives in Scotland, where he has spent most of his life. Yet for more than forty years he has made his career in the study of the Bushmen or San and is one of the world's experts on these peoples. His early field research was in Botswana, and he has also done fieldwork in South Africa and in Namibia. He served as an Honorary Consul of Namibia for eleven years, with the main responsibility of fostering educational links between Namibia and Scotland. In 2010, he was elected a Fellow of The British Academy. He has written more than a dozen books, including ones on the Naro language, on the Khoisan peoples of southern Africa, a children's book on Bushmen, an academic book on the same topic, and a book on anthropological interpretations of Bushmen. He also writes on human origins and on the history of anthropology. His books have been translated into some eighteen languages.

****

THE BUSHMEN (SAN) OF AFRICA

Contents

Preface	1
Introduction	3
The Kalahari Environment	15
The Many Groups of Bushmen	29
Society: The Complexity of Life	39
Culture: How to Share	47
Religion and Worldview	55
Finally, Learning	65
The Future	69
Questions for Discussion	77
Sources and Suggestions for Further Reading	79
Films	89
Glossary	93
About Hearing Others' Voices	99
Join the Hearing Others' Voices Community	103

****

THE BUSHMEN (SAN) OF AFRICA

Preface

What is a 'Bushman'? Is the very word demeaning, or is it a word one can take pride in? I think it is the latter, and in this book I will explain why. The theme of the book is education, and that really is a complex topic. When I lived in the Kalahari, I learned a great deal. Some of what I learned is similar to book knowledge: about botany and zoology, the seasons, time, the environment, and so on. Some was really esoteric: about kinship, religion, politics, economics – all the things that make up any human society. What struck me the most is how we are all human, and that the essence of our humanity is to be found in everything we, as humans, do.

The idea of a 40,000 year span of time is not new; it is the estimate made by an eminent Italian archaeologist. The material culture of Bushmen is very similar to what has been found archaeologically in several parts of southern Africa. Indeed, the archaeologist in question (Francesco d'Errico) reckons it is at least 44,000 years. Likewise, the Israeli geneticist Doron Behar gives a date of 40,000 years (in the female line) for the divergence of Bushmen from the rest of humanity. (The date for the male line – father's, father's, father's, father's, father's, etc. – is considerably longer!) Humankind as a whole was traditionally assumed to be about 200,000 years old, although recent work puts the origin, in Africa, at around 315,000 years.

I would like to thank the editors, not least for thinking up this marvellous series. The book and others in the series are intended mainly for the young, but I think everyone can learn, as I did, from the simple yet complex way of life that Bushmen have. I am also indebted to Julie Grant and Graham Hamilton for providing two of the photos.

Alan Barnard

THE BUSHMEN (SAN) OF AFRICA

Introduction

Why do we study the Bushmen? Well, they are interesting. Not just that, but they have a lot to teach us. The first humans existed around 315,000 years ago. They were Africans. We know this thanks to some careful studies by archaeologists, palaeontologists, and geneticists. Some of these have been quite recent, for example a paper published in the journal *Nature* in 2017. If humans have been here for that length of time, what were they doing? How did they live? Did they even have language? Did they have religion? Did they teach their young? Were they violent, or were they peaceful? These are some of the big questions, and in this book we will learn how to answer at least some of them.

What do we know about Bushmen? Actually, 'Bushman' is a problematic word. In the eighteenth century, the word 'Methodist' was similarly problematic. Christians in the Church of England regarded 'Methodism' as ridiculously methodical. However, Methodists, as they came to be called, thought otherwise, and the name stood. Today many people don't like the label 'Bushman'. They prefer to use the term 'San' instead. (San is meant to be pronounced with a long 'ah' for the 'a'.) But remember: neither 'Bushman' nor 'San' are Bushman (or San) words! 'San' was reinvented in the 1970s on the grounds that 'Bushman' was thought to be derogatory, or possibly sexist. The female equivalent, by the way, is 'Bushman woman' (not Bushwoman). Today, both terms are in use, and there is disagreement both in academic circles and among Bushmen themselves about which term is better. And which is worse: Bushman or San? Indeed, as Kuela Kiema suggests below, there are other alternatives, such as 'Kua', which is used parts of the south-eastern Kalahari. Some academics prefer 'Bushman', and others prefer 'San'. Similarly with Bushmen or San themselves. There is no single correct term, and preferences vary.

The Bushmen or San

'San', usually in its masculine plural form, 'Soaqua', 'Saoqua', 'Sanqua', etc., dates from 1653. 'Bushman' (in Dutch, *Bosjesman*) dates from a few years before that, and in these early times Bushmen were commonly called 'Hottentots' – a word that is definitely taboo in southern Africa! But let a Bushman or San have a word here. This scholar, Kuela Kiema, is a member of the Dcuikhoe (or G/wi, G/ui) ethnic group, and he is a graduate in sociology and an accomplished musician. Bushman words often contain 'click' sounds. An explanation of how to pronounce them will be given shortly. He writes (in English):

> If I meet a Tswana or other Bantu I say I am a Kua or a Mosarwa, but if I meet a Naro or any people of my people I refer to myself as a Dcuikhoe. When speaking Setswana, I call myself a Mosarwa, but when speaking English I use the term Bushman or San.

Sound confusing? Tswana are the major ethnic group in Botswana, literally 'the land of the Tswana'. Their language is called Setswana, which is a language within the great Bantu language family, just as English, along with French, German and Sanskrit (among many others) is in the Indo-European language family. Mosarwa just means 'Bushman' in the Tswana language. Note that Kiema uses either Bushman or San. He continues that he doesn't mind whether the terms are popular in academic fields or not. He adds, 'I am a Kua not a San.' 'Kua' is actually another word for 'Bushman' and is popular, especially in the area where G/uikwishe (to give his language its correct name) is spoken. Naro (also called Nharo or Naron) is another ethnic group label, and this is the language I spoke when I lived in the Kalahari Desert. Many !Xoõ also speak Naro as a second language; in fact, typically a San can speak several different languages. However, they will not know how to read or write in *any* of them. The ability to speak is much more important to Bushmen than the ability to write.

Photo 1. A group of Bushmen or San taking shade

In short, there is no easy way out. In the nineteenth century there was much debate on what to call a Bushman, and one writer noted that to call someone a 'San' is rather like calling him or her a 'vagabond or rascal'. And the writer was a native speaker of what we now call *Khoekhoe*, a language closely related to (but not the same as) many Bushman languages. Kiema notes that a San is actually a person who picks up food from the ground or out of a dustbin. You are getting the idea: there is *no correct* term, no word for 'Bushman' in any Bushman language, and they speak a huge variety of *different* languages. Only a very few speak Khoekhoe.

'San' is derived from the Khoekhoe language and is not a San word either. So, in this book, I will usually use the English word *Bushman*. It is worth noting that there are different dialects in several languages, but as a whole they speak not one language or dialect, but a multiplicity of different ones, and each is more different from each other than, say, English is from Sanskrit!

Occasionally, I have used words like *Kua* or *Basarwa* (the plural of *Mosarwa*), and very often *San*. It depends on whom I am speaking to and on what language I am using.

THE BUSHMEN (SAN) OF AFRICA

Probably the best thing is to use a specific word, like Naro, G/wi or Ju/'hoansi, but those only work if we want to address or describe a specific person or the language that they use. Ju/'hoansi is already plural (that's what the -*si* means: *plural*). And in truth, Sān (or more correctly *Saan* or Sān) is actually a common gender plural form, the singular of which would be *Sāb* (pronounced *Sāp*) for males or *Sās* for females. Don't get me started!

We know who the San are, the traditional hunter-gatherers of southern Africa, and the word 'Bushman' ('Bushmen' in the plural) is in my own language. For these reasons it makes sense to me if I use it, at least most of the time.

Which term do you think is the best? Why? But don't be taken in by supposing that 'San' is better simply because you have not heard the word before, or because you might think it is a word in a San language.

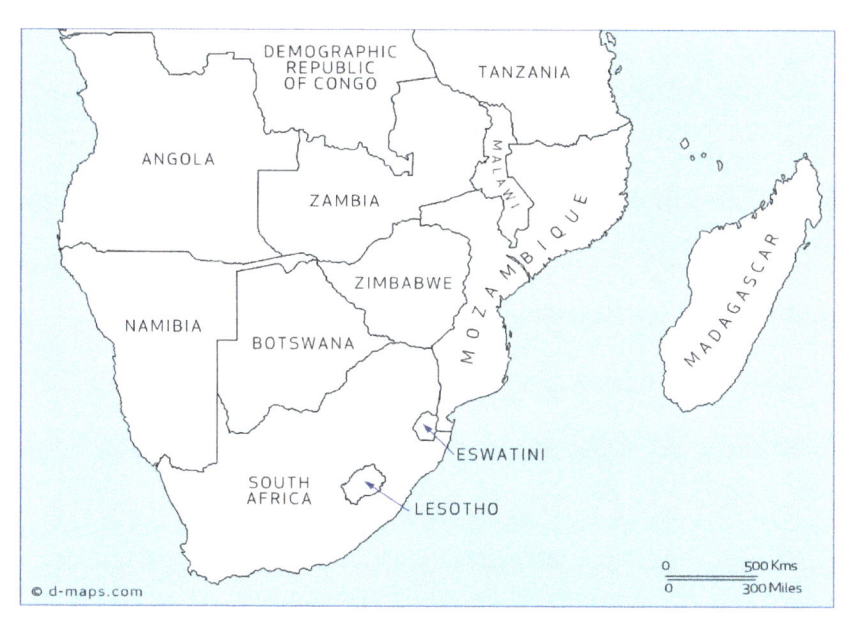

Figure 1. Map of southern Africa

INTRODUCTION

How many Bushman (San) languages are there?

Well, *how long is a piece of string?* Consider this: I mentioned language families earlier. Languages constantly change, but *slowly*. Over hundreds of years, they change quite a bit. Over thousands of years, they change even more. A whole language family, consisting of numerous languages, has a duration of only around 10,000 years at most. So Naro, for example, is not related at all to its northern neighbour, Ju/'hoan. Nor to its southern neighbour, !Xoõ. It is related, however, to its eastern neighbour, G/wi (G/uikuishe) because these languages, Naro and G/wi, belong to the same *language family*. It is a bit like the similarity between English and French. So after, say, 40,000 years, Bushmen or San will have been speaking dozens of different languages, with hardly any similarities among them.

Human beings began in Africa. That is, we humans evolved as a species on the African continent. More than this, when humans first went to live on other continents we took with us everything that first made us human. Did you know that human diversity is basically African in origin? This means that the variation among all the human 'races' is greatest *within* Africa itself? And the biggest difference happens to be *among Bushmen*. They are about as different from each other, in origin, as one 'race' is from the next. The apparent similarities came from the mixing of groups. Forty thousand years is a long time, and since then all the 'races' of the world have been mixing.

So, all in all, throughout history there have been a great number of Bushman languages. Those that still survive are but the tip of an iceberg. All Bushman languages have click consonants, but in other ways they are very, very different: for example, some put the subject first in a sentence, then the verb, then the object (like English). Others put the verb at the end (like Japanese). Of course, there can be variations, but that is the *basic* word order.

Clicks

You might already have noticed some strange spellings! Bushman languages, and some other languages of southern Africa (Zulu, Xhosa and some others) have what we call *clicks*. These are consonants that we *breathe in* on, as opposed to *breathe out* on. Here are the basic click sounds, generally put in order from front to back of the mouth.

- ⊙   The 'kiss click'. Pucker your lips, and then *suck in* a kiss.
- /   Like saying 'tisk tisk' (but just one 'tisk').
- ≠   Written as a 'not equal to' sign, pronounced as a sharp sound with your tongue just behind your teeth.
- // Pronounce it twice, // //, to make your horse go faster!
- !   Like pulling a cork from a bottle or a tab from a can of soda.

For example, say ⊙*wa* ⊙*wa*. That means 'baby' in !Xoõ (Southern Bushman). Of course, very, very few Bushmen are literate, so these symbols were invented by German linguists in the nineteenth century. Also in the nineteenth century, another system of writing clicks was invented, this time by Scottish linguists.

This is the system used for writing the Nguni languages, in which there are just three clicks: c (equivalent to San or Bushman /), x (San //) and q (San !). For example, the word *Xhosa*, the language spoken by the late President Nelson Mandela, has the second one of these, written X.

Bushman languages also have 'tones', like Chinese. So, in Naro, for example, /*am* means 'sun', but /*am* with a slightly different tone can mean a kind of bean. The difference is that the first /*am* has a high tone, and the second one has a low tone. You will notice that the first letter of G/wi is 'g'.

That just means *use your voice* when you say it. There is, in many Bushman languages, extreme grammatical complexity. Naro has dozens of different ways to say 'talk', and it has a great many parts of speech. We mustn't think that these are *primitive people*. They do have primitive technology, but in other ways they are just as sophisticated as you and me!

Population statistics

Some population figures are given in Table 1. A word of warning though! It is difficult to make estimates because we don't know who is to be counted as one. Is *any person* who lives only by hunting and gathering to be counted? What about a *part-time* hunter-gatherer? What about someone whose ancestors hunted and gathered, but who now lives a settled life. Speaks English, rather than a Bushman language? Is only half, or one quarter Bushman? Does she count as a Bushman?

Bushman group
Northern (e.g., Ju/'hoansi, ≠Au//eisi) 10,000
Central (e.g., Naro, G/wi, Shua) 29,000
Southern (e.g., /Xam, !Xoõ) 6,500

Other groups
Nguni (e.g., Zulu, Xhosa) 24,000,000
Sotho (e.g., S. Sotho, Tswana) 21,000,000
Shona 17,000,000

Table 1.
An example of Bushman and other populations in southern Africa.

These population statistics are extremely rough, but one gets the idea: there are *very* few San in the world. Many other peoples are much more numerous, and of course there are mixed populations too – like the so-called 'Coloured' people (those of mixed heritage) of South Africa and neighbouring countries. In South Africa, by the way, *San* is the favoured term for those of 'pure' descent.

The complexity of the Bushman situation is illustrated by examples, like this. The Eastern ǂHoan are a 'Northern' group of Bushmen who live in the south. Believe it or not, the Western ǂHoan are actually an *unrelated* group!

Then there are the Hai//om, a 'Central' group who speak Khoekhoe, the language of the Nama and Damara cattle herders who live in the west. And the 'River Bushmen', a 'Central' group who live in Okavango Delta in the far north. They not only hunt and gather, but also fish for a living. For these sorts of reason, many experts no longer use the traditional labels 'Northern', 'Central' and 'Southern', but complicated labels like 'Khoe-Kwadi', which unites the Khoe (Central Bushmen) and the Kwadi (the virtually extinct San of southern Angola, who once *did* speak the Kwadi language). If all this sounds confusing, *it is*, even to experts!

INTRODUCTION

Always refugees?

Do you know what it's like living in another country? Imagine you had to do that for your whole life.

Well, how do you think the national boundaries of African countries came into being? In 1884, a group of 14 powerful, mainly European countries got together in Berlin. Among them they divided up Africa! This bit for Britain, that bit for Germany and so on. Why do you think the boundary between Botswana and Namibia is a straight line, running north to south?

The point is that natural boundaries were mostly ignored. East of the line was to be British, and west of the line was to be German. In modern times, present-day states have inherited the same boundaries. But think how this might have affected Bushmen. The boundary ran right through the middle of the land of the Ju/'hoansi and the Naro.

Not only that, but the land of the G/wi in central Botswana, was declared part of a 'game reserve'. The G/wi or their ancestors had lived there for thousands of years. Now they were forbidden to live on their own land. Eventually, crossing places were put in across the Namibia/Botswana border to allow Ju/'hoasi to cross, but the Botswana situation was more difficult. Twice, G/wi were forced to leave their own lands. But here too, after some long court cases, a compromise was reached: the G/wi could return to their own territory. They did not have to be refugees forever! But at least at first, they were denied other things, like the right to water and the right to hunt.

The struggles of the G/wi are well described in Kuela Kiema's book, *Tears for My Land*.

'Remote Area Dwellers'?

In the Tswana language there is a phrase, *tengnyanateng*. Literally, it means 'deep inside deep'. Yet, as one expert put it, Basarwa (to use the Tswana term) are not really 'deep inside deep'; it is Gaborone, the capital city, that is *tengnyanateng*.

Botswana is among the best governed countries in all of Africa. Unlike many other countries, Botswana has free and fair elections. It is also at least among the richest, possibly *the richest* on the continent. This is because its economy is based on three things: diamonds, cattle, and tourism. Diamonds are pretty obvious, and cattle very numerous and are exported to many other countries. Tourism is a popular pastime (or at least it was before the pandemic), especially for wealthy people from Western countries. However, the poorest people in Botswana are still the Basarwa. We find their way of life beautiful and interesting, which it is. In Botswana, Basarwa are often called 'Remote Area Dwellers' (RADS forshort), but we have to ask: who is really *remote*?

Is it the Basarwa, or is it *the politicians*? That is the real meaning behind the quotation above.

In recent times, the G/wi and G//ana have been forced to leave their traditional home in the Central Kalahari Game Reserve (CKGR). It has an area bigger than the Netherlands, or twice the size of Wales or Massachusetts. The CKGR has a population today of just 150, and has only ever had a population of fewer than 5,000. Wales has a population of about 3,000,000 and the Netherlands about 17,000,000. Massachusetts has nearly 7,000,000. So what is going on?

INTRODUCTION

Diamonds were first discovered in the CKGR in 1984, and a year later the government declared it uninhabitable by traditional means. Virtually, the entire population was resettled elsewhere. By this time, at least a few G/wi and G//ana had begun herding goats and hunting on horseback. Then there were a long series of court cases, some in favour of allowing the Basarwa to return, and others denying them the right to use the water. Life had become very complicated for these 'Remote Area Dwellers'!

In 2014 it was estimated that a newly discovered diamond mine in the CKGR had the possibility of yielding US $4.9 *billion*! If Botswana is the richest country in Africa, we must ask if these people are really such a drain on the country's natural resources? Enough to forbid *any* hunting at all within the Reserve? Who does 'own' the CKGR? It was created in 1961 for the G/wi and G//ana who lived there. Officially, it had two purposes: to protect the wildlife and to enable the human population to live, as long as they did so by traditional hunting and gathering. This was five years after Botswana gained its independence, and the G/wi had lived there for at least a few thousand years.

Photo 2. A group of Tswana

THE BUSHMEN (SAN) OF AFRICA

The Kalahari Environment

Namibia is drier than Botswana. Indeed, it is probably the driest country in sub-Saharan Africa. The population of Namibia is only about 2.86 people per square kilometre, and about 2,600,000 in total. Botswana is slightly wetter and is the country in which most Basarwa live.

It has a density of 3 people per square kilometre and a total population of around 2,400,000. By way of comparison, Botswana is about the same size as France (65,400,000 population), and Namibia is as big as all the German-speaking areas of Europe (Germany and Austria, and the German-speaking parts of Switzerland) put together. Such very low population densities require lots and lots of land, because in order to live as hunter-gatherers people need much more land than do farmers. And even so, Bushmen are still only a very small population. It is difficult for me to give an exact figure, but there are probably fewer than 46,000 San in the world.

Commonly, we think of the Kalahari as a desert. Yes, it is a desert, but there is an abundance of grass. Cattle keepers have come into much of the Kalahari over the past few hundred years, in order to feed their cattle on this grass. There are also a great many species of plant, but several may be unfamiliar to us: mongongo or mangetti nuts, morama beans, 'Kalahari cucumbers', etc. Mongongos are particularly prized, but unfortunately occur only in a small area in the northern Kalahari. Mongongo is the Tswana name for the plant, and mangetti is the Herero name. Ju/'hoansi call them //"xa. One expert estimates that there are around 220 species of plant and that some of these are unknown to Western botany. Some of these are used in medicines, but the vast majority are cooked and eaten by the human population. According to the UN Food and Agriculture Organization, indigenous peoples' food systems are among the most sustainable on earth. Biodiversity is apparent and through careful management the San can preserve and enrich it. We might ask, what do *we* do in this regard? There is little water for drinking but enough to keep people alive. Remember, global warming is real. The water may be only a spoonful, but it is precious.

What is needed in the Kalahari is *land*. Hunter-gatherers in general need a lot of land to really thrive. It would be impossible to imagine a *city* in the Kalahari (although such a city has occurred in fiction). As long as people can live without luxuries, there is enough space for all, including cattle, sheep and goats. It is just that there is not enough land to support more than a meagre number of people. Another comparison: Australia, which is also very low in population density, has about 3 people per square kilometre. Australia is actually more populous than Namibia. In spite of the population statistics, San are better fed than the cattle herders. When there is a drought, it is mainly the herders who are affected. That is because you need more water to keep cattle than to hunt and gather.

Not only that, but Bushmen don't live as precarious an existence as we might think. Consider the title of the book 'affluence without abundance' by anthropologist James Suzman. Bushmen actually spend *less* time in work-related activities than do their neighbours, the Tswana and the Herero. But of course, it is difficult to measure what constitutes 'work' in an economy that is *not* based on money. Be that as it may, measurements of two or three hours per day in 'work activities' are not unusual.

THE KALAHARI ENVIRONMENT

What is a 'work activity' anyway? Certainly, hunting and gathering, but also hut building, doing beadwork, making hunting equipment, etc., would probably count as work. Think how you might count how much time you spend in 'work'.

Photo 3. *Three men carrying small ostriches and hunting quivers*

Photo 4. *Bushmen in traditional dress*

Wikipedia entry, 'Namibia', accessed 12 August 2021

Climate and social groups

Being a desert, the land is essentially dry. Occasionally it does rain, usually in the southern winter. The rain is usually spotty, a little here and a little there.

Remember that the seasons of the southern hemisphere are the reverse of those in the northern hemisphere. So, it is warmer in January, and colder in June. The longest day occurs in January, and the shortest in June. Bushmen tend to divide the year into five seasons. Of course, the names for them varies according to what language they speak, but it is convenient for us to think in terms of summer wet season (beginning around December) and winter dry season (beginning around June).

The Kalahari is perhaps not really a desert in the strictest sense. There is an abundance of vegetation, but it is mainly grass. Some San can distinguish many different species of grasses. Only the southern area really has very little vegetation. Throughout much of the rest, there are thorn trees and many species of nuts and berries. Most of these are edible, and good use can be made of them. Mainly, they are eaten raw, but there are also many roots and tubers that can be cooked. Land temperatures vary quite a lot. In the summer (roughly, December to March) it is hot both day and night. It can be up to 46 degrees C (or 115 degrees F). In the winter, (roughly, June to September) it is again hot in the day, but it can be below freezing at night. It rains only at the hottest time of year, around November to March or April. When it rains, it can really rain! A heavy downpour is quite common.

It may be difficult to get your head around these facts, but if you think of it, sunrise is, of course, in the east and sunset in the west.

THE KALAHARI ENVIRONMENT

But this means that the sun appears to cross the sky from left to right in the northern hemisphere, but from right to left in the southern hemisphere. As someone who grew up in the northern hemisphere, this once gave me some problems. It also caused the Portuguese explorer Vasco da Gama (1460s to 1524) equal problems, but it *did* prove that he really had sailed around the coast of Africa. The sun appeared to him to be in the *wrong* place in the sky!

Consider how the climate influences social life. Let's take a look at settlement patterns (Figure 2 and Figure 3). Note the difference. The Kalahari is driest in the south, but in the north there is enough water to keep a reasonable population. Therefore, the Ju/'hoansi or !Kung can come together (aggregate) in the dry season.

Ju/'hoansi (!Kung)

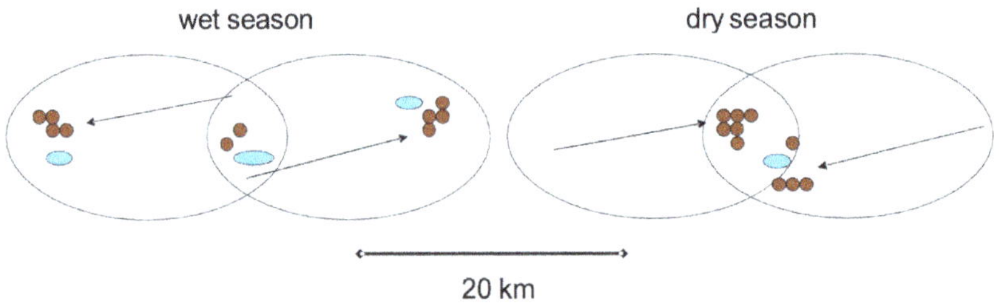

Figure 2. The settlement patterns of the Ju/'hoansi

They do this around the waterholes that are scattered through their land. Note that the diagram is schematic and not to scale. The tiny circles represent individual families, and the ovals represent sources of water. Sometimes these are large pans, but often they are just springs. The large circles, 20 kilometres across, represent the 'band territories', what the Ju/'hoansi call call *n!oresi*.

THE BUSHMEN (SAN) OF AFRICA

The -*si* in the name just makes it plural: one *n!ore*, two *n!oresi*. Similarly, one Ju/'hoan, two Ju/'hoansi. The Ju/'hoansi are exactly the same people as the !Kung. Indeed, many anthropologists still call them *!Kung*.

In this book, the Ju/'hoansi and the G/wi will be my main examples. In Figure 3, one band has left the band territory to find water elsewhere, and this is not uncommon for them. You will gather that the *band* is the main unit of social organization. Each band is headed by a male 'owner' and his wife, or often, and in the case of both Ju/'hoansi and the G/wi, several such owners.

G/wi (/Guikhoe)

wet season   dry season

←——————→
20 km

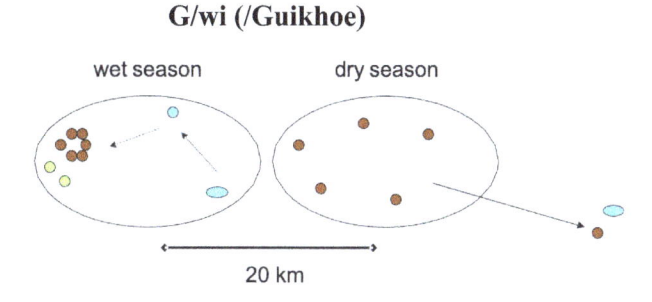

Figure 3. The settlement pattern of the G/wi

Among other groups this may also be the case. Such a title has no real meaning beyond the symbolism of it. Theoretically, in order to hunt in another band's territory, one needs permission of the owners, and since only men hunt it might be assumed that only men can give this permission. Ownership may be inherited from either males or females, and it is different from being either the headman or the chief. Bushmen shy away from such honours, so it can be difficult to know who might be in charge!

THE KALAHARI ENVIRONMENT

Smaller than the band is the *family*, and larger is the *band cluster* or *nexus*. A band can have a population of just a dozen or so, or have a population of twenty or thirty. Historically, bands numbered up to a hundred, but around thirty is typical for Bushman groups today. There is no set number of people in a band, any more than there is in a family. It all depends on environmental resources. Having as many as a hundred occurred for a short time in the 1890s, when there was an epidemic of what was known as *rinderpest* or cattle plague, a cattle disease that swept down through eastern Africa. It was caused by a virus and affected many species. Elephants, in particular, died in great numbers then, and this was the reason so many people were present – to feed on the rotting elephant flesh. It was recorded by a few explorers at the time.

The two groups are rather different; Ju/'hoansi are a Northern group, and G/wi are a Central group. The Northern Kalahari groups are now called Kx'a, this being their language family. The Central groups are called Khoe. These labels are only a few years old, especially in the case of Kx'a, but they seem to be sticking. It seems handier just to call them Central and Northern though. And by the way, there is also a Southern group known collectively as Taa, who live in the southern Kalahari, in the case of the !Xoõ, or farther south in the case of the /'Auni and ≠Khomani. Separate wet and dry seasons are shown. In the dry season there is still enough water as long as families can live. Yet the difference in seasons can be striking.

Photo 5 shows what happens when it is really dry. The footprints are those of cattle, which would normally be present here, on this cattle farm or ranch. I should point out that the Ju/'hoansi the G/wi are only two of the peoples of the Kalahari. They are, however, indicative of a trend. Some groups, such as the Naro, have plenty of water and can live in most any size of camp. Others, such as the !Xoõ can be very short of water. Each group does the best they can in the circumstances, and this flexibility enables them to keep things as they are. Flexibility may indeed be a hallmark of hunter-gatherer lifestyles in general.

Photo 5. River valley in the dry season

Climate crisis

We all know about climate change. But the world right now is experiencing a climate crisis. This means that we are on the verge of experiencing difficulties everywhere.

Islands in oceans far away are in danger of being flooded. The Kalahari is there, but is it in any danger? Will there be enough water for everyone? At present, there is enough water, but will this always be the case? Some experts say it will not be. We already know that hunter-gatherers need much more land than people who grow crops. The G/wi have *very* few resources, but they survive by making the best of what they have. The Botswana government has been trying to force them off their land for a long time. Things are not good for them.

The world has changed a lot since the industrial revolution a few hundred years ago. If there is further change, can Bushmen survive? Can any of us survive? We know that Bushmen share their land with herders of cattle, sheep and goats. These animals all use much more water than humans, and the non-Bushmen are much more numerous than the Bushmen.

THE BUSHMEN (SAN) OF AFRICA

Which way does the river flow?

It depends on the season! The Okavango is a vast inland sea. But it is so flat there that the difference in elevation is almost imperceptible. Theoretically, the Okavango flows from the wetlands in Angola to north, towards the Kalahari to the south.

Angola feeds the Okavango during the Kalahari's *dry* season (May or June to September or October), and the river dries out during the Kalahari's *wet* season (usually, December to March). It's sort of counter-intuitive because the distance is so great – the Okavango is long, 1,200 km from north to south. Rainfall is varied, of course, and droughts are common. About 80 percent of the water is lost through evaporation, and the rest seeps into the ground. And so, there is a vast inland sea that never is empty and never flows into any larger body of water. In this it is unique in the world.

The Kalahari is, in effect, a semi-desert, and some parts are more desert-like than others. The Okavango occupies the area to the north of it, especially the far southern part, is extremely dry, and much of it is fine sand or dust. It is almost too hot to touch, and the sand is full of thorns and not at all like a beach. Bushmen live in societies, but they do this without any form of government. That pretty much does mean without any social hierarchy. And ideally, without violence. Yet some Basarwa groups are thought to be superior to others. Usually, the 'superior' groups are those that have the most food in their territories. Food here really tends to be meat, which is their preference. Traditionally, this is game meat – different kinds of venison as well as small game animals. Typically, the small animals are squirrels or turtles, and the venison includes many species: springbok, gemsbok, steenbok, kudu and so on.

There are also rhinoceros, giraffe, elephant, hippopotamus, and a great many more species. Not all these are edible, but the vast majority are. The anthropologist Richard Lee wrote that Bushmen eat more meat than Texans! In short, they can eat very well indeed.

In addition to game meat, some Bushmen also eat fish. This is especially true in the Okavango region, an area perhaps the size of Wales or of New Jersey in the USA. Bushmen do not eat fish if they can help it: that is a bit like eating snake, some say. Of course, though, such comparisons to areas of Africa or North America are extremely difficult because the size of the Okavango depends so much on what season we are talking about. I have been there when it was flooded, but I have also experienced it dry as a bone. In any case, the Okavango has more than 70 species of fish, and also hippos, giraffe, elephants and so on. It also boasts the Moremi Game Reserve, one of the richest wildlife areas in the world. One of the great contradictions of their way of life is that they endure droughts and flooding, in equal measure and at odd times of the year. And food is often plentiful, especially when they kill a large animal. But it is often not, like when they don't have enough to go around. They burn off the grass, so that more food is produced in the following year, but they also must endure their share of seasonal drought – which, ironically, occurs in the wet season. The rain that feeds it is the rain in Angola, much farther to the north.

THE BUSHMEN (SAN) OF AFRICA

Photo 6 and photo 7 show scenes on the Okavango. In Photo 6 you can see hippos in the background. Photo 7 shows a herd of elephants. I was probably a little too close to them, trying out my new camera. Don't try this at home! It can be dangerous.

Photo 6. The Okavango

Photo 7. A herd of elephants: not uncommon in the Okavango

How climate change may affect this in the future is a difficult story. In recent times, there has been a huge increase in greenhouse gasses, especially carbon dioxide. Ultimately, this was caused by the industrial revolution, which began in the eighteenth century. There is also an ever-increasing need for water, and there has been a greater presence of wildfires throughout the world. These are quite unlike the carefully managed fires in the Kalahari. They occur to burn off the unnecessary grass that threatens the extraction of food plants. In many parts of the world, such as Bangladesh, the encroaching of the sea is a serious problem. The existence of low-lying islands is another. Happily, this does not affect southern Africa, but climate change is a problem for the whole world, both right now and in the future.

****

THE BUSHMEN (SAN) OF AFRICA

The many groups of bushmen

It is common to think of Bushmen as being all the same. In fact, there are a great many different Bushman groups. Consider the different languages. If a *language family* lasts for 10,000 years, how long can a single language last? The answer, of course, depends on what we mean by a language. These change over time. Look at the difference between British and American English, for example. They split just a few hundred years ago. The English of Shakespeare a few hundred years before that. Of Chaucer, a few hundred years more. Old English, or Anglo-Saxon, spoken 1000 years ago, was quite unintelligible to modern ears. And throw in all the influences, like French and so on, it becomes quite complicated! Well, that's what happened with Bushmen.

The first studies of Bushman languages were done is earnest in 1870, by German linguist Wilhelm Bleek. This was in the northern Cape Province of South Africa. But sadly, Bleek (pronounced 'blake') died young in 1875, so his studies were continued by his sister-in-law, Lucy Lloyd. The people were called the /Xam, in the !Wi language family, and the research Bleek and Lloyd did is contained in the thousands of pages of text now held by the J.W. Jagger Library of the University of Cape Town. Not bad for a group of six prisoners employed as gardeners! In fact, as far as Bleek and Lloyd were concerned, they were mainly there, working in the garden, in order to tell folk tales in their own language. Their prison sentences were given mainly for stealing cattle. There was a fire in the library in 2021, but happily the Bleek and Lloyd material survived.

But not so the /Xam language, which died out in the early 1900s.

Bushmen belong to many groups

I once counted the various names of Bushman groups and came up with more than 200! And some of these are not in a place once expected, because of migrations a few hundred years ago. *Forty thousand* years ago, Bushmen were speaking a great many languages. Some of these disappeared. Some merged with others, a bit like the mixing of Norman French and earlier forms of English, to produce Modern English. A small number of words are found in several languages. The word for 'spirit of the dead' for example, is *g//āua, g//ama*, etc. Bushmen tend to live in very tiny groups, and in general they do not know how to write. I once met an illiterate man who could speak about eight or nine languages, in five different language families! His first language was one called N!aqrixe, or Eastern ≠Hoã, which today is spoken by only around 100 people or fewer.

The fact is that Bushmen can speak a great many languages. As the example of *g//āua* above shows, it is difficult to say how many. Some are very similar, but others are so different as to be counted not only as different *languages* (like French and English), but languages within several quite different *language families* (like Chinese and English). With languages dividing every few hundred or a thousand years, it is impossible to know how many languages were spoken in the past. Today we know there are there are languages in just three Bushman language families, for convenience generally called Northern, Central and Southern. Some linguists, though, prefer more technical names, like Kx'a, Khoe-Kwadi and !Wi. Of course, there may have been many more. Probably, all of them were small, and the diversity implied possibly dozens or even hundreds. The distances between any two were no doubt enormous. Southern Africa was a very different place in the past, and we must not think everything was as it is today.

Wage labour and other activities

Eating cattle and, to a lesser extent fish, is not how most people in southern Africa live. In Botswana and Namibia, as anywhere else, the majority of food is vegetable: roots, tubers, berries and so on. San may live quite a hard life, and while men do nearly all of the hunting, women and children bring in the most food. That said, they don't necessarily do more *work* than we in the West! Estimates vary, but it is true that the average Bushman spends less than three hours per day in any kind of work. But what is work? If they don't earn any money, what do they do?

Well, if they want cash, they have to take jobs. Since they have few apparent skills, the possibilities are not great. They can look after someone else's cattle, or they can keep a few goats for themselves. Building a hut can be time consuming, but not as much as building a whole house would be. And in building, both men and women participate. Men do the heavier work of bending and cutting branches, and women do the thatching. Bead work is common among women, and it can be time consuming, for example, to cut and drill holes in small pieces of ostrich eggshell takes ages. This is their favourite form of jewellery and is much prized. Another activity commonly done by women is collecting firewood. However, there really is no discrimination, since almost anything may be done by either men or women. Likewise, children are not excluded, so boys and girls may easily be allowed to join the list and do some work. But again how do we define this work?

THE BUSHMEN (SAN) OF AFRICA

The diet may not be great, but think about it: humans have lived as hunters and gatherers for as long as humans have been on earth, for at least 315,000 years. They have a huge knowledge of their environment. In fact, studies have shown that in bad times, it is *easier* to live by hunting and gathering than by herding animals. After all, herding livestock has only been in existence for around 13,000 years – a much shorter time than hunting and gathering. The reason why agriculture was developed is likely to have been climate change, so the present climate crisis was not the first one. However, it is very different because it is no longer possible for humans *all* to live by hunting and gathering. The population of the world is now way too large for this to be possible.

Equipment is not complicated: bows and arrows, snares to catch rodents, and so on. Some of these were invented long ago, bows and arrows for instance. Where game is plentiful, hunting is not especially difficult. With vegetables as a main source of food and a specialized set of skills, they can use things like water melons, beans and nuts, Kalahari onions or Kalahari potatoes. They may not taste as nice as what we are used to, but there are a lot of them. Don't forget, they really do know the environment. They also know not just how to hunt, but where to hunt and when to hunt, and how to track. Labour is not only in the hands of the poor, but, more or less, in the hands of everyone equally. One expert has even suggested that the *art of tracking* was the very beginning of science. And tracking is important because it is *meat* that is most desired, and not vegetables, berries or nuts.

So, what do they do in their spare time? They play games, like the *parachute game* (my term), or the *melon game*. The *parachute game* just involves flicking a seed with a small branch attached a few metres up, and watching it float slowly to the ground. The *melon game* just involves tossing a melon backwards. It is played only by women and girls. Men and boys would rather hunt instead.

In hunting, Bushmen often use sign language: to speak might frighten the animals. Sharing, as we shall see, is very important to Bushmen, and so too is playing games and playing music. Dancing occurs too, especially in the medicine dance. Also, there is art. In the distant past, thousands of years ago, this involved rock painting as well as engraving. As their lifestyle is much easier than we might think, they have plenty of time on their hands. And things do get easier as time goes on. As generally they do very little work, this should be obvious! The invention of games was just part of life for hunters and gatherers, and so too was art, music and so on.

Photo 8. A man playing the segaba a one-stringed musical instrument

The seventeenth-century philosopher Thomas Hobbes once speculated that 'primitive' humans lived a life that was 'nasty, brutish and short', but it seems that he was wrong! Hunter-gatherers as other 'primitive peoples' are actually better fed than many others. This is partly because they have rich sources of vegetables. These have more nutrition than meat, and game meat is more nutritious than other meat, such as beef. Putting all this together, we humans were better off as hunter-gatherers.

THE BUSHMEN (SAN) OF AFRICA

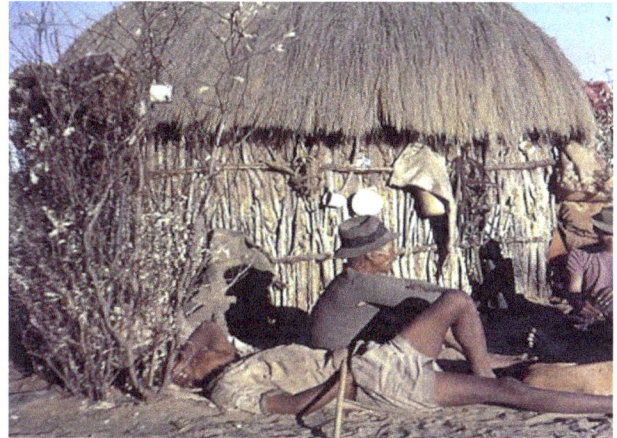

Photo 9.
Not a lot to do!

Photo 10.
A hot dry season camp, Namibia

Photo 11.
A cooler dry season camp, Botswana

The Khoekhoe and others

Related to some Bushman groups, especially the Central ones, are the Khoekhoe. Together the Bushmen and the Khoekhoe are called the *Khoisan peoples*. The Khoekhoe are mainly cattle-herders and a bit more numerous than San. They have lived in southern Africa for a thousand years, rather less time than the San. They keep cattle, sheep and goats, and today some San, when they can afford it, also keep livestock. Europeans first settled in South Africa, specifically in Cape Town, in 1652 – although historians point out that there was contact before that. Although they once lived in South Africa, today most Khoekhoe live in Namibia. In the past both Bushmen and Khoekhoe were persecuted, and some Khoekhoe kept Bushmen as servants. Happily, this is no longer the case. However, Bushmen still have a lower status than any other ethnic group.

Do Bushmen like living where they do? Well, they certainly like having the free time that they do have. But the lack of property is a problem for some. Long ago, there was a common belief that Bushmen were forced to their present locations. The belief was that their territory was always small. However, we now know that this was not quite true. Bushmen were once part of a large collection of peoples that inhabited many parts of Africa. We know this thanks to genetic studies and archaeological research. Archaeologists tend to call them San, just as South Africans do. The inhabitants of most of Africa today are Bantu-speakers, part of a great language family that came down through much of Africa a couple of thousand years ago. These latter groups include peoples such as the Xhosa, Zulu and Tswana, who are all in contact with Bushmen.

Some of their languages even have 'clicks', which they received through years of contact with the San. But remember, the Tswana, Zulu and Xhosa have only lived in southern Africa for around two or three thousand years, and the Bushmen or their ancestors have been there for more than 40,000 years.

All Bushmen were traditionally hunter-gatherers. Some today keep goats or (very rarely) cattle. It is possible, if sometimes difficult, to keep livestock in the Kalahari because there is sufficient grass for them to eat. The main problem for everyone is finding enough water. That is the reason population size, of either livestock or people, has to be small. In Botswana, the country where most Basarwa live, the population is about 2,400,000, and fewer than 3 percent of them are Kua or Basarwa.

We think of the Kalahari as a place for Basarwa. This is true, but they remain very tiny groups. Still, they are diverse groups, often in contact with one another. Their languages may sound similar, since all of them have clicks. Their diversity reflects the great distances between different groups. Their similarities reflect the fact that they have lived in the same part of Africa for thousands of years. They have to an extent copied from each other, even though genetically they are very diverse. Experts have found greater genetic diversity among Bushmen than among any other people on earth. To you (and me) they may all look much the same, but the similarities may hide much more difference than you might think. We do not know the prehistory of Bushmen because it was never written down, but we do know they have lived in more-or-less their present locations for a very long time.

Remember, Bushmen are diverse. They live great distances from each other and speak many different languages. Yet, they are hardly the most numerous of peoples in the Kalahari. Khoekhoe in Namibia, Herero in Namibia and Botswana, Tswana and Kgalagadi in Botswana – and many other groups are just as numerous. Some of these, the Tswana for example, are far more numerous, and there are Tswana in South Africa as well as in Botswana. Bushmen represent only a tiny part of the population anywhere.

****

THE BUSHMEN (SAN) OF AFRICA

Society: the complexity of life

Anthropologists talk a lot about *societies*. In the Americas, anthropologists tend to talk about *cultures* instead. It does not really matter, but do note the plural. There are many different societies or cultures in the world, not just one.

That said, consider this point. Bushman society is, by its nature, *anarchistic*. This means that although Bushmen live in societies, with rules about how to behave, they do this without the intervention of any government! So, is Bushman society peaceful? I would say, very much so.

Somebody might get hurt!

However, an earlier ethnographer wanted to find out if they had a concept of 'war'. She put the question to them, as best she could.

> She asked: 'Do your people ever throw spears at others, or shoot at them with bows and arrows? This might be, for example, to drive them off their land.'
>
> One Bushman interrupted: '*Wait just a minute!* Do *your* people have this custom?'
>
> She answered, 'Yes, sadly, we do.'
>
> 'Well, forgive me', said the Bushman, '*I think this is a very silly custom. Don't you realise, somebody might get hurt!*'

Yes, I think she did realise that. Indeed, this *was* a danger, and actually, it was the point! When the first white people settled in Africa they brought with them their guns and their culture of violence. They took the lands of the Bushmen, and they did this with extreme violence.

It is not just that they drove Bushmen farther north, they killed them in the name of 'sport'. In some cases, they enslaved them. And they put them in prison, a concept that was completely alien to their understanding. What Bushmen do instead is *banish* someone, so they don't cause any more trouble. Theft is not completely unknown, but it is usually pretty obvious who the thief is.

Photo 12. Preparing for a hunt

Violence among Bushmen

Another ethnographer reported on the high degree of violence. It seems that a common threat, even if it is usually a threat, is to suggest using arrow poison on someone. Arrows are commonly poisoned at the tip, and the poison is said to have no antidote. The poison is made from the larvae of a kind of beetle and is necessary. Bushman arrows have no flights, and their bows are quite flimsy. Without poisoning their arrows, they would never be able to kill large antelope or other big game. Sometimes, after shooting it, they have to track an animal for ages before it falls dead.

Bushmen may not have a concept of warfare, but they do have a concept of theft. This may not be as common as we might think, though, because they have few possessions, and what they do not have they can usually make. The threat may come from outsiders, or it may come from other Bushmen. The ethnographer, Richard Lee reckoned that murder rates are higher among Bushmen than in the West. Of course, there are forms of violence apart from murder, but things like hitting someone are not infrequent. Many Bushmen have livestock these days, and stealing livestock is becoming increasingly common. How do they manage? Well, there are no doubt contradictions here. They do not recognise war, but there is violence. Theft exists, but it is not felt to be right. There are, of course, no prisons, although outsiders (normally governments) do frequently throw San into jail. Can it be right that Bushmen or San can live without the restrictions imposed by governments? And without paying any taxes? At all! Obviously, this is a point for debate. Left on their own, they are peaceful. Outsiders are the problem.

There is a debate already about whether hunter-gatherers should have to pay to live under a government, any government! Bushmen have been called the anarchists of the Kalahari. I suppose they are, but should they be exempt from living under a government that they have no part in? After all, they are (whether they want to be or not) citizens of the country that claims them. They do pay to go into hospital, but the fees for that in Botswana are minimal – literally 10 South African cents (less than a US penny) when I was living there in the 1970s. The point of having *any* fee at all was just to discourage scroungers.

Society and culture

Bushmen have culture. In fact, they have *cultures*. Although there are a great many similarities among them, I use the plural to suggest that there are differences, especially in language and in kinship practices.

The word *society* suggests a concept that is common in Europe and in parts of Africa and Australia. In North and South America, reference is usually to *culture* instead. It does not really matter: these concepts just reflect differences in how anthropology is taught, whether through American influence (culture) or British influence (society). If it is any more complicated than that, think where the words come from: culture from German and society from French. (And American anthropology began in the late nineteenth century, with several German immigrants importing German ideas.)

So what are these differences in language and in kinship practices? Language is simple and has already been covered: languages change over time, and Bushmen have been living in

Africa for a very long time indeed. Kinship is a little different. Without getting too much into the technicalities (my own specialized interest has always been in kinship), let's just say that they classify their relatives quite differently. For example, the Ju/'hoansi have what is called a 'lineal bifurcate collateral' system, and the Khoe-speaking peoples, Naro, G/wi and so on, have an 'Iroquois bifurcate merging' system. What this means is that Ju/'hoansi call their relatives with terms like uncle, cousin and so on (just as we who speak English do). Naro, G/wi and other Khoe-speakers or Central Bushmen instead distinguish *different kinds of* aunts, uncles and cousins. For example, both my mother and my mother's sister are called 'mother', and their children are called as *different kinds of* cousin.

The details don't matter for now, and they really only matter to Bushmen themselves (or, of course, to those who study them). The point to remember is that we must never take anything for granted. The 'Iroquois' way of classifying our cousins is not only found among the Iroquois people of North America; it is in fact the most common way of classifying relatives worldwide! *Most* peoples in the world have 'Iroquois' kinship terminology.

THE BUSHMEN (SAN) OF AFRICA

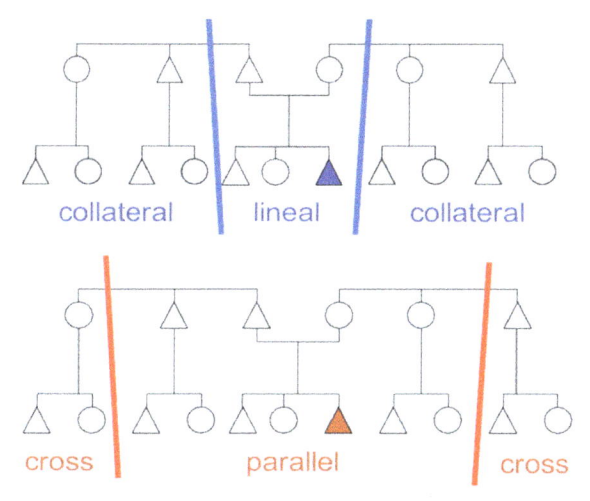

Figure 4. How Bushman classify their relatives

Figure 4 shows the difference between the two most common ways Bushmen classify relatives. In English, we use the lineal/collateral distinction. So do the Ju/'hoansi. But it is more common worldwide to make a parallel/cross distinction. This is what the Central groups, like G/wi and Naro, do: they distinguish the parallel cousins from the cross-cousins. The former are called *as if* 'brother' and 'sister'. In the diagram, males are represented by triangles, and females by circles. This is the way anthropologists label their diagrams.

By the way, it doesn't matter if someone has fewer or more than one brother or sister, since the circles and triangles represent *hypothetical* relatives. Anthropologists just assume one of each. This all tends to confuse anthropology students, and is the reason that in this kind of diagram we always draw it in exactly the same way, without regard to the age of the cousins. The one coloured in is the one who is known as *ego* (meaning 'I' in Latin), the person we are tracing from.

The top row, for example, shows, from left to right, my father's sister, my father's brother, my father, my mother, my mother's sister, and my mother's brother: one of everything! And *just* one. This matters because what we are trying to show is the way relatives can be classified.

In English, as in Ju/'hoan, all is clear: cousins are all cousins. In G/wi or Naro, however, *my father's brother* is not considered a cousin at all but a kind of 'father', and *my mother's sister* is a kind of 'mother'. Of course, people do know who their *real* relatives are. It is just that how they classify them is entirely cultural.

Summary

Bushmen have no concept of war, but they do have a concept of violence. They are anarchists, because they do not recognize government or why governments should be needed. But they do live in societies, and indeed they are social beings. These facts are important, and they should challenge many of our suppositions about what it means to live in a society. For this reason, it is good that we study a people like the Bushmen.

Studying them helps us to understand ourselves better. Even things we take for granted, like classifying our relatives, are different in different parts of the world. Should we learn to live more like they do? That is up to you and me. We will find out more when we take on what it means to *share*.

****

THE BUSHMEN (SAN) OF AFRICA

Culture: how to share

Anthropologists tend to talk about culture quite a lot. This is perhaps especially true in North America, where *culture* has overtaken *society* as a fundamental concept. The two, though, can be thought of as basically the same. A lot of customs are just invented and eventually copied are passed on. Let me take an example, possibly a trivial one. Bushmen tend to walk in a long line, one person after another. Elsewhere, such as in America or China, people usually walk in pairs or in a bunch, side by side. Ever thought of why this is the case? I'm not really sure, but I know it is true. I suspect part of it simply is custom. The practical reason, though, is fear of snakes. They might be there; one never knows. But if we keep together in a column it is far less likely that we'll run into snakes. Or if we do, only the first person is at risk!

Sharing, talking and giving

One of the most famous articles ever published by an anthropologist was called 'Sharing, talking and giving'. It was written in the 1950s by Lorna Marshall. All cultures or societies have values. In Bushman societies, perhaps the most striking is sharing. The custom in many Bushman groups is to lend your arrows to others. The person makes a kill is *not* the owner of the arrow, because he loaned it to another. The owner is the one whose arrow makes the kill. This is one of the many Bushman customs that serves to equalize the distribution of property. The custom is to give meat, but it isn't really your own meat, but always someone else's. Yes, it is not quite the same thing as socialism, but in a sense, it has the same effect. It redistributes the wealth of the group.

THE BUSHMEN (SAN) OF AFRICA

In Bushman society, sharing is very, very important. It serves to spread the wealth, so that nobody has too much or too little. Consider the place of sharing in hunter-gatherer ideology in general. That said, only meat is shared. There are very strict rules for this. For example, a hunter will give the best part of the meat to his parents-in-law and inferior parts to others. Vegetable food is not shared: you have to find it yourself. This part of Bushman culture is pretty much the same from one area to another.

Figure 5 shows a general explanation of sharing and how Bushman society differs from Western custom. Our own society values the accumulation of property, whereas Bushman society values giving things away. Which custom do you think is better?

Bushman culture
(sharing is valued)

sharing of food	appropriate behaviour
accumulation of food	anti-social and selfish

Western culture
(accumulation is valued)

storing food and property	appropriate behaviour
immediate consumption	anti-social and selfish

Figure 5. The value of sharing

Bushman ideology favours giving, rather than the creation of wealth. It downplays competitiveness. Our society is just the opposite. As for the killed animal, it is much the same. At least among the Ju/'hoansi, the largest of the Bushman groups, there is a belief that when an animal is killed it gives up its *n/om*. This is believed to be a substance that is found everywhere. It is released whenever an animal dies. In humans, it is released at birth. Every creature has it.

CULTURE: HOW TO SHARE

So, if Bushman ideology favours giving, you might ask, how does anyone ever get rich? That is just the point. Bushmen *don't want to get rich!* They would rather give things away. Perhaps I should add, they would rather *be seen to give things away.* I remember when I lived in the Kalahari, people would often own two tobacco pouches: an empty one to show other people, and a full one in which to hide your tobacco! People might know you had more tobacco, but to display it would be wrong.

This attitude sort of accounts for the strange custom of 'inverse *mafisa*'. But in order to understand it, you first need to know what *mafisa* is. *Mafisa* is a Tswana custom. Wealthy people give poor people some of their livestock in exchange for poor people looking after their herd. Usually, the wealthy are Tswana, and the poor are Bushmen. So, what is 'inverse *mafisa*'? This is when a poor person *loans* his livestock to a rich person to look after. The rich person is seen to have wealth, but it doesn't matter. It is like putting your money into a bank, and paying the bank interest to look after it! Why would you do such a thing? The same reason as you might have two tobacco pouches. It not how much wealth you have that counts, but how much you *appear* to have.

This custom was discovered by anthropologist Thomas Widlok in northern Namibia, among the Hai//om Bushmen and their wealthier neighbours, the Ovambo.

THE BUSHMEN (SAN) OF AFRICA

*Photo 13. Part of a wet season village
(the back hut is in Tswana style, but the front two are more typical
for Bushmen)*

Bushmen and the microwave oven

Did you know the story of the microwave oven? It was invented in the 1940s and is based on radar technology. A technician was trying out a radar device, while in his pocket there was a chocolate bar. The bar melted. Eventually, the first 'radar cooker' was made.

However, to make a success of it, the price had to come way down, and the oven had to be made in an affordable size. The earliest microwaves cost thousands of dollars, and early ones would take over your kitchen! No-one could afford one, and the company that first made them tried to interest the US navy, railway companies and so on. Nobody wanted to buy it. So, the microwave did not become commercially successful until the 1970s.

What were the inventors to do? Well, the founder of the company that had invented them, Laurence Marshall, had an idea. Tired of making weapons of war, he sold his company and used the profits to take his family on a very long holiday. When Marshall and his wife Lorna asked their friends if they could find something useful to do, they were told about *anthropology*. Biological subjects were 'too difficult' and 'technical'. And so, Lorna Marshall became one of the greatest ethnographers of all time! She spent years studying the way of life of the Ju/'hoansi, who came to be known as the !Kung. The whole family was involved. Son John became famous as a documentary film maker, and daughter Elizabeth Marshall Thomas as a writer on the 'harmless people'.

All this because of the failure to sell a microwave oven!

Universal kinship

One of the most striking features of any Bushman society is *universal kinship*. I am proud to say that I 'discovered' this around 1974. However, I didn't really *discover* it at all because Bushmen had known about it all along – probably for millennia!

I named the phenomenon 'universal kinship'. The name was not, I suppose, the best of label, but it did stick. In universal kinship, there is no such thing as 'non-kin': everyone is related to everyone. Unlike Australian Aborigines though, Bushmen do not take this to the extreme of including their dogs! Universal kinship for Bushmen is only for humans. But it does work for *all* humans, even for outsiders. The way it works is like this: every human has a name, even anthropologists and some other outsiders, such as people who speak Bantu languages.

When I lived with the Naro they gave me the name *!A/e*, which is fairly common (about as common as *Alan* is, in the English-speaking world). If I meet another person with this name, I call him my *grand-relative*. Names are gender-specific, so he will be male.

Then supposing I meet his sister. What do I call her? Well, she will be my 'sister', and the two of us should not have sex with each other. That would be 'incest'! so this is not thought of as hypothetical or metaphorical kinship, because it is 'real'. Unlike for instance a 'father' in the Catholic church or a 'brother' in the trade union movement, this is 'real' kinship because it regulates our behaviour. It is just as if we were a real brother and sister and not an anthropologist and his friend! Anyone I meet can be placed in a kinship category, according to his or her name. So, Bushmen are my 'sisters', 'brothers', 'parents', 'children' and so on. This happens among the Naro, the main group I worked with.

Incidentally, among the G/wi it works in a similar way, but among the Ju/'hoansi it is entirely different. This is a key difference between Central Bushmen (like G/wi and Naro) and Northern Bushmen (like Ju/'hoansi). The latter classify their relatives a bit more like English-speakers, distinguishing 'lineal relatives' from 'collateral relatives', rather than 'parallel relatives' from 'cross-relatives'. Yet they also have a peculiarity that astonished the Marshall family. Their cousins are sometimes called as if uncles and aunts, and vice versa – if they are named after them! Enough about kinship!

Love and marriage

We tend to think that love and marriage go together. In fact, our association between these two concepts is relatively recent – only over the last few hundred years. Do you know that what we today regard as normal behaviour is pretty much the norm in Bushman society too? Since they have little wealth, there is no notion of marriage for money. In fact, Bushmen have very little notion of marriage at all.

The exception is the Naro, who have quite elaborate exchanges of gifts upon marriage and upon the first child born to a couple. Also fairly unusual is the giving of 'bridewealth'. Normally this is something to be expected among herding populations, but both Naro and Ju/'hoansi practise it. It is very possible that Bushmen have picked up this idea from their neighbours, but it is usual among several groups for small gifts to be given at marriage. These are not big gifts, but rather just tokens – remember, Bushmen do not have much wealth, in cattle or anything else. They do sometimes have a few goats, and Bushmen could have got the idea through owning them.

Also, people do not know how long they will be married. A trial marriage is quite permissible among either Naro or Ju/'hoansi. In fact, the idea of being a girlfriend or boyfriend seems to blend seamlessly into being wife and husband, and residence is commonly with the wife's group at first, and then later to the husband's. A final note: marriage among some groups is traditionally by 'capture'. This means that boys 'take' their brides. I would not read too much into this though. It is just a tradition among several groups, and it may even reflect what was done in the distant past.

In Western societies, people might have several sexual partners, then get engaged to one of them, and then marry. It is much the same for Bushmen, except that they don't actually get married! Still, partnership for life is pretty common. They don't exchange rings, but the idea of a lifelong commitment is regarded as normal. So is the idea of having just one partner, or at least one partner at a time. In other words, Bushmen behave much like the rest of us. Occasionally though, people do marry more than one person at a time. Divorce occurs, and jealousy is not uncommon.

Photo 14. A baobab tree

Religion and worldview

All Bushmen have a knowledge of religion. This is not to say that they have a clear understanding of *what* they believe or believe in. It is sometimes useful to distinguish between *physical* medicine and *spiritual* medicine. The former is pretty obvious: it's like what you can get at the pharmacy. The latter is more akin to religion. Worldview is similar, like the way you understand the world or the universe.

In fact, music, art, morality and religion have been around for a very long time. They existed long before people knew about anything else. Language too is very, very ancient. There are theories about this. For example, in the nineteenth century a common idea was that dreams came first, and that religion reflected what people dreamed about.

Gods and goddesses

I pointed out earlier that a common word in many languages is *g//āua*. This is the spirit of a dead person. But in some languages, this term is easily translated as 'Devil'. Especially in G/wi I have heard it used as such. Sometimes the Great G//āua is opposed to the High God, who is called N!adi, or to specify that he is male, N!diba. Some say that there is a female equivalent, N!adi-sa. (In some languages, *ba-* is the masculine suffix, and *sa-* is the feminine.) It is sometimes said that 'God' has many names, a little like the idea in Islam. This is true for the Ju/'hoansi, for example. Naro say that God *is* 'the Sky' (both are called N!adiba), but that his *name* is Hieseba.

There is no single San religion, and the views of individual San or Kua vary. They do not generally disagree on such matters though, since nobody would claim to know the nature of the spirit world any better than anyone else. In these and many other things, Bushmen tend to be modest. If you don't know something, it is best not to speculate.

In some Bushman belief systems, especially in the south, God is associated with the moon. For this reason, early ethnographers referred to one group, the //Xegwi, as 'moon-worshippers'. Often (but not always) the moon is said to be 'good', and the sun 'bad', and the moon is *male* and the sun is *female*. This is the opposite of European languages. For example, in French the moon is described using the feminine gender (*la lune*), while the sun is masculine (*le sol*). Of course, there is nothing 'natural' about this, and in Europe we do not think of heavenly bodies as being good or bad. Possibly, 'bad' here might simply refer to the warming properties of the sun: in the Kalahari, it is often very hot! Yet it is just as likely that it simply relates to the vagaries of gender languages. There is no real reason why one thing should be hot and another cold. Indeed, among hunter-gatherers in general, the genders are the reverse of what we in the West usually think of as the 'natural' order of things: male sun and female moon in the West or the northern hemisphere, the reverse among Bushmen. However, this could simply reflect the fact that hunter-gatherers tend to live in the southern hemisphere and non-hunter-gatherers tend to live in the northern hemisphere.

Bushman religious beliefs are different in different parts of southern Africa, and in some Bushman groups there are differences of opinion about what is true.

Even questions like 'How many gods are there?' has no meaning! Think of the comparison with Christian belief: are 'father, son and holy ghost' the same being or three different ones? Sometimes Bushmen talk about there being one god, N!adi-ba (in Naro), but then bring in the idea of his wife, Nadi-sa or even his two wives, N!adi-sara. Of the two wives, one is said to be the 'mother' of the moon and sun the next day, or one the 'mother' of the moon and the other of the sun!

For this reason, it is difficult to pin down exactly what Bushmen believe in. My answer is that it doesn't really matter. There is no 'correct' Bushman theology: Bushmen believe whatever they wish to believe, and one can get many different answers, sometimes even from the same person. Bushman theology, as in discussing seasons, is flexible and adaptive. In the /Xam language (which is no longer spoken by anyone), the word for 'God' was not *G//āua* but */Kaggen*. This word also means 'mantis', a kind of stick insect that is supposed to have magical properties, and the two concepts (God and mantis) are seen as identical. Such are the strange ways of Bushman belief. In several Bushman languages, there is no difference between a myth, a tale one just heard (for example, about a hunt) and a true event: in the Naro language, they are all just *hua-ne*, or in the singular, a *hua*. I would translate this as 'story'. Of course, the Naro *do* know the difference, but which it is does not really matter much. I once heard a Naro *hua* which turned out to be the myth of the Tower of Babel! This did not matter at all to the person telling it.

THE BUSHMEN (SAN) OF AFRICA

Rituals

Among many groups there are two important rituals: the *medicine dance* and the *girl's initiation ceremony*. Sometimes there is also a *boys' initiation ceremony*. Where the latter exists (for example among the !Xoõ, at least in the past), it is usually held in a collective way: several boys at the same time. That particular ceremony is dying out. Even the !Xoõ no longer generally have a ceremony for boys, and sometimes simple hunting magic replaces it. This involves a boy getting small cuts, a bit like tattoos, between his eyes. These are said to help him 'see' his prey. But what this means in practice, it is difficult to say. Things like this do change through time. And Basarwa are so open to change, that pretty much anything is possible. Possibly this is the reason that Christianity has in recent years become so common among Bushmen? Obviously, this has been especially true at mission stations, like the Kuru Development Trust, in D'Kar, Botswana.

The girl's initiation ceremony is more clear cut than the male ceremony. It is held when the girl reaches puberty, and also is specific to that girl. A girl's initiation is usually quite a sombre event, marking the girl's first menstrual period. Among several groups, the women of a band dance in a figure-of-eight around the fire, with no men (except the 'eland') present. They flip their dresses behind them as they dance. The 'eland bull' is generally the only man permitted. He dances behind the women, and he symbolizes male sexuality. Ideally, you need a real eland's horns, but if you don't have them, two fingers above the head will do! This is the sign of the eland in hunting sign language. All the while, the initiate sits alone in her hut.

RELIGION AND WORLDVIEW

Photo 15: A medicine dance
(Photo by Julie Grant)

She leaves only when necessary. Occasionally, there are 'rude' songs, with boys jumping in – once I heard boys trying to sing the girl's initiation song, for example! Photo 15 shows the beginnings of a medicine dance. No one is yet in trance, but give it time. Trance is no doubt an exhilarating experience. A man may achieve unusual sights, typically reporting seeing snakes, lions, and shooting stars. I suspect these are not real though, but brought on by a kind of altered state of consciousness. It is like what one might see when taking drugs. On the other hand, strange things do happen to men in trance. I once observed a man in trance swallowing nine hot coals. Later, I asked how he had felt. Perhaps predictably, he said he had felt hot inside! For this reason, entering trance can be difficult, and not every man has this ability. And only a smaller number of women seem to have it. The power of trance has been likened to 'boiling', and the power to that of a jet engine. This ability seems especially common in parts of the northern Kalahari, particularly among the Ju/'hoansi.

I would not claim to have ever been in trance myself, but at least one ethnographer has made this claim. The number of Bushmen who would claim to being able to achieve trance varies from one in three people to, perhaps, one in eight or ten. I have heard of women being able to do this too, but in women it is very uncommon. Mainly, trance is for men only. Going into trance is a bit like being a wizard, perhaps easy if, like Harry Potter, you are born one, but otherwise something you have to train to do. No wonder there is an article on the subject called 'Education for transcendence'. It was written by Richard Katz, a psychologist and psychological anthropologist who once watched how it is done and wrote about it. The important thing among the Ju/'hoansi is activate your *n/um*. This is a sort of magical substance that does 'boil' within the medicine person. Some people have it, and others simply don't!

When in trance, men tend to wear cocoons strapped to their legs. These make noise as the men dance. This is because the cocoons are filled with stones. In general, women do not dance. Instead, they sit and sing accompanying songs. The songs are often traditional and well known. From time to time they change though, as when the Giraffe Dance was invented among the Ju/'hoansi. Usually, a song lasts just a few minutes among the Ju/'hoansi, but ten or twenty minutes among the Naro. It will have a clear ending, but often no clear beginning. That is, sometimes women begin to sing, but if no men dance, the attempt fizzles out. I have seen about twenty or thirty medicine dance beginnings, but only about twenty, if that, carried to completion. Some Bushman groups are better than others at performing medicine dances, especially in the northern part of the Kalahari. Mostly, dances are held around full moon. This may be for practical reasons, since

RELIGION AND WORLDVIEW

seeing what is going on can be crucial. It also depends on how many people are present. A good medicine dance needs at least a few dozen people. Occasionally, if someone is really ill, a medicine dance may be held on the spur of the moment. Or if someone is possessed by a wandering spirit! I saw this once, but I gather that it is very rare. New dances are invented as needed, as there is no set routine about this.

As we see in Photos 16 and 17, artwork is a common pastime. There are two kinds, and both are very ancient: painting and engraving. Sometimes art depicts scenes from nature; sometimes it is more abstract. Photo 17 obviously depicts a couple of zebra (as would be said in southern Africa) or zebras (as would be said elsewhere). More abstract art may depict, for example, what someone might 'see' when in a trance.

Photo 16.
Artists at work

Photo 17.
Rock engraving

Worldview: how many gods are there?

Worldview is simply a wider way of looking at the world. In this I would include religion in the conventional sense. But it might also include a general attitude towards what is out there. Healing is important, as is a sense of community. Healing is also for everyone: nobody is excluded. Even strangers (and even anthropologists) are 'healed' in the same way as Bushmen. There are many phases of healing in a medicine dance, and each is taken in turn. And no one gets special treatment: not good hunters, not especially esteemed people, but only perhaps pregnant women. People are healed according to need.

Bushmen are known for their modesty. This is why they are not dogmatic about what they believe in. They do not claim a knowledge of the spirits or of their world. But community is very important to them. They tend to accept what is common knowledge. I noticed in my own fieldwork that the two most common phrases seem to be: 'God wills it' and 'I don't know'. In a sense, these sort of mean the same thing. It is an explanation of almost anything one doesn't understand. Note that I just used the word 'God'. Does this mean that they are monotheistic? Well, sort of ! Throughout much of Africa there tends to be an assumption that there is a single god, although people also talk as if there are many of them. Certainly, they have a notion that there are spirits out there and that these spirits can be evil.

I know this is a difficult concept for us to get our heads around. I did once write an article about this in a religion journal. I think the theologians understood it, but I'm not really sure if I did myself ! The notion that the high god is married to another entity or has children is kind of irrelevant.

This is because *the Bushman god is not really a countable thing.* Basically, they do believe in a single god; it tends to be non-Bushmen, like the Greeks and Romans, who believe there are many gods and goddesses.

In short, Bushmen have a different understanding of the world than we do. It is not better or worse; it is just different.

******

THE BUSHMEN (SAN) OF AFRICA

Finally, learning

One of the most awkward moments of my field research was in explaining toilet paper! Or rather, trying not to explain it. A Bushman cleans his or her bottom with grass. One day, a young girl asked what a roll of toilet paper was for. She knew I took notes quite often, but obviously the small round bundle could not be for taking notes on! So, what was it for?

There is a lesson here. We cannot explain everything we do. Nor is everything oblivious to a stranger. That's why anthropologists exist. In thinking about this trivial example, we must never forget that this is true in all societies. A Bushman may speak several languages, often very complicated ones, but even what is obvious to you and me may not be obvious to them.

Learning about plants and animals

I probably know the names of, maybe, a hundred plants and animals. And I only know these in English, or perhaps a few in Latin too, if I think about it. But a Bushman will know about many hundreds more.

Bushmen today live mainly in Botswana and Namibia. There are Bushmen too in South Africa, and some in other southern African countries, including Zambia, Zimbabwe, and Angola. There were once Bushmen in Lesotho as well, and a rock art expert once produced a poster that urged modern people to remember those who had lived before. There are none left now in Lesotho, but fragments of their luxurious rock paintings are still there. Remember too that Bushmen once inhabited the whole of southern Africa, even if today they are confined only to the remotest desert regions. Do they have an interest in parts of the world they have never seen? In geography, for example?

In fact, often they do. Geography might seem a strange interest, but that is what interested !Xoõ the most when I once asked them. They had never seen an ocean, but when I told them about oceans, they expressed a great interest. Don't imagine that education is only for those who have book learning; it is really for everyone – even the poorest of the poor. Even people who never travelled. It is similar with botany, and for science in general. They have a knowledge of a great many plants and animals, and often they want to know more about them. Many Bushmen have a knowledge that would astound Western scientists. But for their lack of education, they would be scientists themselves. Or would they? Actually, two things might hold them back. One is, frankly, laziness. Study of course takes time, which they do have, and effort, which they may have. But how would that work in this 'original affluent society', where free time is valued more than hard work?

This contradiction is difficult for many an anthropologist to handle. Bushmen know as much about plants as a botanist, as much about animals as a zoologist, as much about rocks as a geologist …. But can they turn this understanding into knowledge? That is a dilemma.

Of course, learning is continuous. During my time as an Honorary Consul of Namibia, a small group of Bushmen visited me at my home in Scotland. They were performing as dancers at one of the festivals and we posed beneath the Namibian flag. It is at present a great rarity for any Bushman to travel abroad, though in the future this may change.

Travel is beyond their means, though not beyond their wish. Maybe in the future. It was summer, but cold, even for me. They spoke mainly Ju/'hoan and some other Bushman languages, and I spoke no Ju/'hoan. We were able to communicate in Naro, which I do speak a little bit. Lunch consisted mainly of meat. It was a learning experience both for them and for me.

Photo 18.
A group of Bushmen at the author's home in Scotland
(photo by Graham Hamilton)

THE BUSHMEN (SAN) OF AFRICA

The future

Prince Charles once wrote: *'The Bushman is the essence of Africa ... We all lose if the Bushman disappears.'*

It is worth remembering that Prince Charles studied anthropology at university, along with archaeology, before taking his degree in history. Similarly, his son Prince William studied anthropology along with geography, before moving on to art history. There are many instances of presidents, prime ministers and members of royal families who have studied anthropology, and at least a few who has been practising anthropologists. Indeed, the Bushman presence is there too: Prince Charles's godfather was Sir Laurens van der Post, whose series *The Lost World of the Kalahari* (1956) was the most popular programme on British television prior to the Queen's Coronation in 1953. And Prince Charles once donated a Land Rover to the charity First People of the Kalahari.

Why does this matter? I hope to have shown throughout this book that, although they may be very few in number, Bushmen are still here. Their way of life as non-literate hunters and gatherers, is still viable. Generally, they have little interest in politics, although people did take sides in the Namibian war of liberation. Some conservatives went with the South Africans, and more liberal people tended to favour SWAPO (the South West Africa People's Organisation). SWAPO was the former independence party, although wearing a SWAPO t-shirt is not necessarily an indication of allegiance! (T-shirts were given away for free.) They have a great deal to teach the rest of us, for example, about avoiding the horrible effects of climate change.

Tens of thousands of years of learning about the environment and how to make the most of it should not count for nothing. I have met a few really wise people, and I am sure some of the wisest *are* people who know how to live off the land, without livestock, vegetable stores, supermarkets or even shops of any kind. Some of the wisest are, in fact, Bushmen. I may be able to speak a couple of languages, but never in my wildest dreams could I be able to speak nine or ten. Bushmen can, and many of them do.

The great structuralist anthropologist, Claude Lévi-Strauss, once explained his strategy like this: '... what we are doing is not building a theory with which to interpret the facts, but rather trying to get back to the older native theory at the origin of the facts we are trying to explain'. Sounds a bit difficult to get your head around, but what he meant was that humankind is a couple of million years old, and that he saw no reason to assume that people like Plato or Einstein were not solving difficult problems long ago. It's just that they had different problems to solve, like questions in kinship theory! I suppose I can do that, but which is more useful: kinship theory, botany, or languages? I hesitate to think.

Will the Bushmen survive?

In my book *Bushmen: Kalahari Hunter-Gatherers and Their Descendants*, I asked 'Will the Bushmen survive?' The short answer is, of course they will. But times change, and people do too. Think of the /Xam. Did they really disappear? Not really. They became the *Karretjie Mense*. This means, the (Donkey) *Cart People*. They are wandering sheep shearers of South Africa, who have taken to travelling around, communicating by way of mobiles (cell phones) to find the next flock of sheep that need shearing. They know that their ancestors were the /Xam, but today they speak Afrikaans (which is related to Dutch). So, they have survived, but not quite in the way we might think. But in another sense, have they? Are the wandering sheep shearers of South Africa *really* the same people as the /Xam?

At the moment, there is a pandemic. Throughout the world people a dying of SARS-CoV-2, the virus that causes COVID-19. A different virus, however, is afflicting Bushmen. This is HIV, which gives people AIDS. Perhaps because of sexual promiscuity, this seems to affect Bushmen more than other people. And when they become ill, they will generally not have access to the anti-retroviral drugs that they would need to combat the illness. AIDS is very common among Bushmen, and is rife in general in southern Africa. Health organizations are doing their best to fight AIDS, but there is almost nothing that can be done. Unfortunately, without literacy and a population that remains 'remote', what can be done?

Namibia, specifically its Ministry of International Relations and Cooperation, maintains a policy of being 'being friends to all, and enemy of none'. It was also the first country *in the world* to have protection of the environment written into its constitution. That was in 1990, when Namibia gained its independence from South Africa. Botswana also has a good record of free elections and friendship to the outside world. It became independent from the United Kingdom in 1966. However, among the richest countries in Africa, it has not always been kind to Bushmen, or Basarwa, as they are called in the country. The long-running court battles have shown this. Their future will be different from the one they had hoped for, but it is still a future.

Germany tried to kill every Herero then alive around 1904, but they failed. 'Ethnic cleansing' does not ever work.

Figure 6 shows the Coat of Arms of the Republic of South Africa. It shows two Bushmen clasping hands and is said to mean 'Diverse people unite'.

Figure 6. *Coat of Arms of the Republic of South Africa*
Wikipedia entry 'Coat of arms South Africa', accessed 9 August 2021

More literally it means something like 'People who differ are coming together, talking to one another'. The meaning of *//ke* is little ambiguous: it can mean 'unite', or it can mean simply 'talk to each other'. (The macron in *e:* just means that the *e* sound is long.)

Since /Xam is no longer spoken at all, by anyone (except a few scholars), that is about the best we can do. But what a good motto for a young country!

So, the population that has lived almost longer than any other on earth, purely by hunting and gathering, is in trouble. But it is a resilient population that has learned to adapt before.

So, when do we stop learning?

I have been studying Bushmen for more than forty years, and I am still learning. Some of my knowledge comes from my reading, in other words what my colleagues are writing about them. Some comes from new Bushman words I pick up.

Still, in spite of good intensions all is not well. South Africa became a democracy in 1994, but it too has problems with its relations with San, as they are usually called in that country. Many South African San are actually from Angola and fought on the South African, pro-apartheid, side in their war leading up to free elections. They were actually members of the South African National Defence Force (31 Battalion). But we must ask, which side would they be on now? Are they for freedom, or for apartheid? I believe they are now on the side of freedom, and have regretted being part of the regime that once supported apartheid. Yet how can we know? What were liberal-minded people to do when Namibia earned its freedom, and with only four years to go until democracy came to South Africa? And yes, Namibia was affected by apartheid just as much as South Africa; South Africa took control over Namibia from the United Nations Mandate (inherited from the League of Nations Mandate) from 1915 until Namibian independence in 1990. This is because Namibia had once been German Southwest Africa, and German colonies in Africa were divided up as Mandates given to other countries to control. It was all very complicated!

What happened was that the South Africans established a place for Bushmen or San to live. It was called Schmidtstdrift, and is still there on a site near the famous diamond mines at Kimberly.

THE BUSHMEN (SAN) OF AFRICA

At first there were about 4,000, divided between two groups: one an Angolan group called the !Xun, who are related to the Ju/'hoansi. They numbered about 3000, including both fighters and their dependants. The other group were the Kxoe from the Okavango, and distantly related to the G/wi. They numbered about 1000. Today the population of Schmidtsdrift and its extension, called Platfontein, has a rather larger population.

Nothing inspires hope more than being resourceful. Nothing is more useful than being comfortable. We can see, for example in Photo 15, how useful it is to have fire. Fire was first used perhaps two million years ago, not by *Homo sapiens* but before that, by our ancestors. It enables us to keep warm at night (it is often very cold in the Kalahari), and also to make to make tools. It is culturally important too, simply to gather around in a medicine dance. It is central, for that reason if no other, to sustain the Bushman way of life. It is less important in modern society of course, where it is often replaced by a television set.

Has the TV really replaced the fire? I would say it has. But just as humans have found new ways of adapting, we have found new things to adapt to. Fire is one; perhaps the computer and the mobile telephone would be others. That's how adaptation works.

****

THE BUSHMEN (SAN) OF AFRICA

Questions for discussion

1. What term do you prefer, and why? San, Bushmen, Basarwa, Kua, southern African hunter-gatherers, southern African foragers …?

2. What do you make of the epigraph in Richard Lee's *The !Kung San*? It is: '*Why should we plant, when there are so many mongongos in the world?*'

3. Would you like to live like a Bushman? Affluent, but with little work to do? Or would you rather work hard?

4. What do you think of Bushman religion? Freedom of thought, or nonsensical?

5. Climate change: is it real?

6. How would you recognize a Bushman? By what he wears? By the language she speaks?

7. What about a Donkey Cart Person: in the nineteenth century, she would have been a Bushman. Can she be thought of as that today?

8. How many languages can you speak? How many can you read? I'll bet you speak more than you can read. Most Bushmen can only read languages they speak, but this may be half a dozen or more! Why do you suppose some people still refer to them as 'stupid Bushmen'?

THE BUSHMEN (SAN) OF AFRICA

Sources and suggestions for further reading

Introduction

The quotation is from:

- Kuela Kiema, 2010, *Tears for My Land: A Social History of the Kua of the Central Kalahari Game Reserve, Tc'amnquoo*, Gaborone, Botswana: Mmegi Publishing House, page 67.

There are also a number of revealing books about the very bad treatment of Bushmen or San in the past. For example:

- Sandy Gall, 2001, *The Bushmen of Southern Africa: Slaughter of the Innocent*, London: Chatto & Windus.

A few of the books are my own, and the difference lies in the intended audience. Let me put them in order from 'for younger readers' to 'for academic readers'. Some, particularly *Kalahari Bushmen*, are very well illustrated. That one also shows the difference between traditional life and modern, usually through the photos.

- Alan Barnard, 1993, *Kalahari Bushmen* (Threatened Cultures) Hove: Wayland Publishers. 48 pages. Target audience: ages 11 to 14. There is actually a separate edition in the United States, on the supposition that the American and British linguistic traditions are so different!

- Alan Barnard, 1978, *Bushmen* (Discovering Other Cultures), London: Museum of Mankind, 16 pages. Just a short booklet, also for general readers.

- Alan Barnard, 2022, *The Bushmen (San) of Africa: 40,000 Years of Learning*, London and Singapore: Balestier Press. (*This book!*)

- Alan Barnard, 2007, *Anthropology and the Bushman*, Oxford / New York: Berg Publishers. This one is really mostly about anthropology and its understanding of Bushmen.

- Alan Barnard, 2019, *Bushmen: Kalahari Hunter-Gatherers and Their Descendants*. Cambridge: Cambridge University Press. 206 pages. A scholarly book, intended mainly for academic readers.

- Alan Barnard, 1992. *Hunters and Herders of Southern Africa: A Comparative Ethnography of the Khoisan Peoples*. Cambridge: Cambridge University Press. 349 pages. Another scholarly book. Deals with both the Bushmen and the Khoekhoe.

Another book very much worth reading is:

- Megan Biesele and Kxao Royal /O/oo, 1997, *San* (The Heritage Library of African Peoples), New York: The Rosen Publishing Group. Biesele has many years' field experience with the Ju/'hoansi and speaks Ju/'hoan very well, and /O/oo is school teacher who collaborated with Biesele on several translation projects.

The Kalahari environment

The best ethnographic treatment of Bushmen and the environment is:

- Richard Borshay Lee, 1979, *The !Kung San: Men, Women, and Work in a Foraging Society*, Cambridge: Cambridge University Press. This book is good, but note: it is also very long, 526 pages.

There are few books directly about the Kalahari, but let me just mention two and a more general book on climate change. They are very different though. Aloian's is a short, prize-winning children's book. Thomas and Shaw's is a long, academic book (and fairly old). Brooke provides a more up to date account of climate change in general. It is written by a historian. What these books have in common is the notion that the Kalahari is not really a desert as we normally think of one.

- Molly Aloian, 2012, *The Kalahari Desert* (Deserts of the World), New York: Crabtree Publishing Company.

- David S. G. Thomas and Paul A. Shaw, 1991, *The Kalahari Environment*. Cambridge: Cambridge University Press.

- John L. Brooke, 2014, *Climate Change and the Course of Global History: A Rough Journey*, New York: Cambridge University Press.

Although not really a desert by some measurements, the Kalahari can be very hot and very dry. Photo 3 shows this. Figures 2 and 3 are, of course, schematic. I have used them before, and they are based on several sources.

THE BUSHMEN (SAN) OF AFRICA

There are, of course, many books about climate change. A good place to start is with:

- Bill Gates, 2021, *How to Avoid a Climate Disaster: The Solutions We Have and Breakthroughs We Need*, London: Allen Lane. It describes the situation in quite a personal way.

Or, again, if you'd like a historical view, try:

- Benjamin Lieberman and Elizabeth Gordon, 2018, *Climate Change in Human History: Prehistory to the Present*, London: Bloomsbury. There is good coverage of hunter-gatherers, but there are quite a lot of footnotes.

The many groups of Bushmen

Among the first ethnographers of the Bushmen were:

- W. H. I. Bleek and L. C. Lloyd, 1911, *Specimens of Bushman Folklore*, London: George Allen & Company. The date may be ancient and the style unusual, but it contains a great many texts in both the /Xam original and in English translation. Folklore is very important to Bushmen, not least because it reminds them of their connection to the past. Bleek died in 1875, and Lloyd completed his research.

- D. F. Bleek, 1928, *The Naron: A Bushman Tribe of the Central Kalahari*, Cambridge: Cambridge University Press. D. F. (Dorothea) Bleek was the daughter of W. H. I. (Wilhelm) Bleek. In this short book she describes the way of life of the Naro, also known as the Naron or Nharo. Why so many names?

It depends on gender and on whether you want to hear the breathy sound after the 'n'. (I myself have changed from the earlier spelling *Nharo*, to the modern *Naro*.)

In recent years, there has been a resurgence of interest in Bushman languages. However, pretty-much only highly specialized studies have been published. And the names of the various groups have been changing! The only thing I can advise here is to look at recent work, for example my *Bushmen: Kalahari Hunter-Gatherers and Their Descendants*.

Society: the complexity of life

One of the best books about any Bushman group is:

- George B. Silberbauer, 1981, *Hunter and Habitat in the Central Kalahari Desert*, Cambridge: Cambridge University Press. It deals with the G/wi and especially about ecology. A word of warning, though! You can see how old it is, and a lot has changed since 1981. So, for an update you will need to read a book like Kuela Kiema's *Tears for My Land*, published in 2010.

Among the hundreds of other books published about Bushmen, the most comprehensive is:

- Richard B. Lee, 2013, *The Dobe Ju/'hoansi*. The one to read, if you can find it, is the fourth edition. The international version is published by Wadsworth Cengage Learning and is 294 pages long. It includes Lee's famous essay, 'Eating Christmas in the Kalahari'. This is a warning against the arrogance of one who gives but expects to be congratulated for their generosity.

THE BUSHMEN (SAN) OF AFRICA

(For reasons of copyright and the peculiarities of publishing, this edition is not available in the USA, Canada or Australia.)

The original name of *The Dobe Ju/'hoansi* was *The Dobe !Kung*. It was changed when *Ju/'hoansi* became standard term. Dobe is just their location in the northern Kalahari

Other useful sources include:

- Elizabeth Marshall Thomas, 1959, *The Harmless People*, London: Secker and Warburg.

- Elizabeth Marshall Thomas, 2006, *The Old Way: A Story of the First People*, New York: Picador.

- Marjorie Shostak, 1981, *Nisa: The Life and Words of a !Kung Woman*, Cambridge, MA: Harvard University Press.

- Marjorie Shostak, 2000, *Return to Nisa*, Cambridge, MA: Harvard University Press.

These are all non-fiction, but they read a little like novels. Elizabeth is the daughter of Laurence and Lorna Marshall. Thomas's *The Harmless People* is a great classic. It tells of the family's arrival among the G/wi in 1950. Elizabeth was only nineteen at the time. Her later book tells of their work with the Ju/'hoansi, fifty years later.

Culture: how to share

A key ethnography of sharing is the one by

- Thomas Widlok, 2017, *Anthropology and the Economy of Sharing*, London: Routledge. Widkok has field experience among hunter-gatherers in both southern Africa and Australia, but he looks at the issue in a worldwide perspective. (Widlok, incidentally, wrote the foreword for my earlier book, *Hunters and Gatherers: What Can We Learn from Them*, Balestier Press, 2020.)

There are a great many books about human evolution, but let me mention here just two:

- Gregory Cochran and Henry Harpending, 2009, *The 10,000 Year Explosion: How Civilization Accelerated Human Evolution*, New York: Basic Books.

- Richard L. Currier, 2015, *Unbound: How Eight Technologies Made Us Human, Transformed Society, and Brought Our World to the Brink*, New York: Arcade Publishing.

Neither of these books deals explicitly with Bushmen, but there are references to them in many places. Harpending has done field research with the Ju/'hoansi.

Other books in which sharing is quite prominent are:

- Megan Biesele, 1993, *Women Like Meat: The Folklore and Foraging Ideology of the Kalahari Ju/'hoan*, Johannesburg: Witwatersrand University Press /Bloomington: Indiana University Press. Not only about meat, but about things like the medicine dance, women, and power. Biesele is a specialist in folklore, and her writing style is excellent.

- James Suzman, 2017, *Affluence without Abundance: The Disappearing World of the Bushmen*, New York: Bloomsbury. A good read, by another excellent writer.

Essentially, he argues the case of Marshall Sahlins, who in 1974 argued that free time (affluence) is more important than having more than you need (abundance).

- James Suzman, 2020, *Work: A History of How We Spend Our Time*, London: Bloomsbury. A very thought-provoking book. Quite lengthy though, at 444 pages. Suzman's fieldwork was with the Ju/'hoansi, and this comes through.

- Marshall Sahlins, 1974, 'The original affluent society', in *Stone Age Economics*, London: Tavistock Publications, pages 1-39.

Religion and worldview

A key general ethnography is:

- Lorna Marshall, 1976, *The !Kung of Nyae Nyae*, Cambridge, MA: Harvard University Press. Many would say this is the very best of all Bushman ethnographies. Still, it ignores religion.

But on religion, see:

- Lorna Marshall, 1999, *Nyae Nyae !Kung Beliefs and Rites*, 1999, Cambridge, MA: Peabody Museum. Here at last, she takes on religion. This is the best book on this topic, and it rivals Lee's work in general ethnography.

- Richard Katz, 1982, *Boiling Energy: Community Healing among the Kalahari Kung*, Cambridge, MA: Harvard University Press. Specifically deals with trance performance.

Finally, learning

Rather than directing you to *books* on learning, let me just mention one film.

- *Learning Bush Skills from the San Bushmen of the Kalahari.* This film and many other films are available on YouTube. See under 'Films', below.

The future

The quotation from Prince Charles is from:

- Sandy Gall, 2001, *The Bushmen of Southern Africa: Slaughter of the Innocent*, London: Chatto & Windus, pages xvi-xvii.

The quotation from Claude Lévi-Strauss is from his article in:

- Richard B. Lee and Irven DeVore, 1968, *Man the Hunter*, Chicago: Aldine. Lévi-Strauss's article is called 'The concept of primiveness', pages 349-352, and the quotation is on page 351.

Lee's ethnography is mentioned above. It is very comprehensive and a good place to start. Also very useful are the ethnographies by Lorna Marshall. Remember, !Kung is the older name for the people now generally called Ju/'hoansi.

The Japanese tradition is represented by a number of anthropologists, including especially:

- Jiro Tanaka, 2014, *The Bushmen: A Half-Century Chronicle of Transformations in Hunter-Gatherer Life and Ecology*, Kyoto: Kyoto University Press / Melbourne: Trans Pacific Press.

Again, don't be put off by early dates:

Lee worked with the Ju/'hoansi for many decades from the 1960s to very recently, and Marshall's work began in 1950. Her work also ran for decades, until her death in 2002. She lived to the age of 103, and as we have seen, her children also participated in the family's field research.

****

Films

There are many films about Bushmen. I have already mentioned one, about learning. General introductions to Bushman culture and society include these ones. Some are about Botswana, and others are about Bushmen in Namibia and South Africa. See if you can guess which country they refer to. In some of the films you will hear Bushmen speaking. In this case, see if you can guess the language. Usually it will be Ju/'hoan, but not always. Many of these films are political, in the sense that they refer to struggles between Bushmen and outsiders. This is especially true of *A Kalahari Family*. That is in fact a five-part series which features John Marshall (1932-2005), son of Lorna Marshall (1898-2002) and brother of Elizabeth Marshall Thomas (born 1931).

- *A Kalahari Family*
- *Bushman: Once We were Hunters*
- *Last Song of a Kalahari Bushman*
- *Bushmen of the Kalahari*
- *Bushmen of Botswana*
- *The Controversial Relocation of Kalahari Bushmen*
- *A Kalahari Language – !Xóõ*
- *Kalahari Bushmen San Dancing*
- *How Are the San Bushmen in Namibia Really Like*
- *The Difficult Choice Facing Young Bushmen*
- *A History of the San People*

This is only a sample of some of the best, but there are more. Suggestion: have a debate with your friends. Which one *is* really the best? Why? Because of its accuracy, or because of its depiction of a lost way of life? Or of life in the present? Of the exploitation of the Bushmen in the past?

Finally, what should *we* call *them*? Bushmen, San, Saan, Basarwa, Khoe, Kua, Ju, etc. are just some of the possibilities. What about 'traditional southern African hunter-gatherers'? Or indeed, '… gatherer-hunters' (favoured by some feminists, on the grounds that gathering accounts for more food than hunting)?

Ask yourself, do we need any such term at all?

****

NOTES

THE BUSHMEN (SAN) OF AFRICA

Glossary

Probably, you will know many of these words already. Don't be put off in learning new words. Rather, consider how many you do know.

Afrikaans	Once known as 'Cape Dutch', this is a common language in South Africa and one of its 11 official languages.
affluent	Wealthy.
anarchy	Without government. Typically, Bushmen have no government, although they may have leaders.
anthropology	Sometimes called 'the science of humankind'. It includes human biology, social orcultural anthropology, prehistoric archaeology and anthropological linguistics. The subdisciplines are defined slightly differently in different countries, for example in the US, *cultural anthropology* is the usual term, whereas in the UK it is *social anthropology*.
apartheid	In the past, a system of controlling people by keeping then in separate groups according to 'race'. This was especially true in southern Africa.
archaeology	The study of the past, normally through digging up what is left behind.

THE BUSHMEN (SAN) OF AFRICA

Basarwa — Bushmen. This is a traditional term used in Botswana. Their languages are sometimes grouped together and called *Sesarwa*, but in truth there are many such languages. *Sarwa* is the root, and *Ba-* and *Se-* are prefixes.

borehole — A narrow and very deep hole through the sand. It is drilled to extract water or other liquids from deep under the surface.

bridewealth — The custom of paying from husband to wife upon marriage (the opposite of dowry). In southern Africa, the payment is usually in cattle.

dancing rattles — Rattles that are worn on the legs when men dance. They are filled with stones and make a percussion sound

deities — Gods and goddesses.

dialect — Like a language, but a smaller unit, for example, different kinds of English: Scottish, American, etc.

ecology — The study of the relation of between people and their environment.

egalitarian — The idea of being equal in wealth and status.

epigraph — A short quotation at the beginning of a book. It is meant to hint at its theme.

ethnic cleansing — An attempt to destroy an entire population, and their culture. Examples of perpetrators include Germany, in the War of 1904-05,

GLOSSARY

	the Nazis, and arguably whites against Bushmen in the nineteenth century.
ethnographer	The kind of anthropologist who documents the way of life of a people. For example, Lorna Marshall was an ethnographer of the Ju/'hoansi.
field research, fieldwork	Studying behaviour 'in the field', that is, on site. It often involves working in the local language and generally takes at least a year.
foraging	Another term for hunting and gathering. It is frowned upon by many because, it is said (for example in Japan), *people* hunt and gather whereas only *animals* forage.
genetics	The branch of biology that studies genes, heredity and so on.
Herero	A cattle-keeping group of Namibia and Botswana. Especially in the early 1900s, they were persecuted for their lifestyle.
Homo sapiens	Modern humans. In this sense, all existing human beings (including Bushmen) are 'modern'.
hxaro (*xaro*)	Traditional Ju/'hoan form of giving in delayed gift exchange. It is found among some other groups too, but not found everywhere among Bushmen.
indigenous	Aboriginal, belonging to a specific place.
Kgalagadi	A cattle-keeping group of Botswana.

THE BUSHMEN (SAN) OF AFRICA

Khoekhoe   A traditional group of herders of southern Africa. Their language is called 'Khoekhoegowab'. (At one time they were called 'Hottentots', but that term is no longer regarded as polite.)

Khoisan   Literally, *Khoi* (Khoe or Kxoe) plus *San*. This is the traditional term for these peoples, collectively, and has been in use since the 1920s.

language family   A group of related languages. They share a common origin. The opposite is called (in German) a *Sprachbund*, a group of languages that have *become* more alike, e.g., through constant borrowing of words.

mandate   The authority to control a territory, for example when South Africa was given control over South West Africa, later Southwest Africa (modern Namibia), during the First World War.

mongongo   A seed that grows abundantly, but only in limited areas in the Kalahari.

'race'   An artificial notion of genetics that distinguishes people according to, for example, skin colour. The term was once very common, but today no longer in use within genetics.

shaman	Wizard. This is the general word in anthropology for such a person, who has the ability to enter a state of trance.
structuralist	An anthropologist whose theory depends on *relations between things*, rather than on the meaning of things themselves.
taboo	To be avoided, because using the word may seem unpleasant.
trance	An altered state of consciousness, like in a dream or after having taken drugs.
Tswana	A cattle-keeping people of Botswana. The name of the country means land of the Tswana.

****

THE BUSHMEN (SAN) OF AFRICA

About hearing others' voices

Hearing Others' Voices is a transcultural and interdisciplinary series edited by physicist Roh-Suan Tung and anthropologist Ruth Finnegan for Balestier Press (Singapore and London). It is designed, in simple and straightforward language, to inform and engage general readers, undergraduates and, above all, young adults/school sixth-formers to reflect on who and where they are and to explore recent advances in thought, unaccountably overlooked areas of the world, and key issues of the day.

The series provides accessibly introductions, often fully illustrated, to the latest insights into such perpetual topics as mental health, sounds of the universe, storms, voices of the Christian west, dance, our awesome minds and bodies, and more. They also reveal something of the wisdom of the too often dismissed traditions of, for example, Native America and Africa, bringing a wider understanding and ownership of who and how we and the world have come to be as they are.

Though everyone can enjoy and learn from them, the books are particularly suitable for young adults' school and personal reading and a perfect resource for mind-opening sixth-form general studies. They are designed to stimulate curiosity and provide the material and the insights to start filling important gaps in awareness. The suggestions for further material for those who want to take their understanding further will be an invaluable tool for readers, including those at or preparing for university or examining possible careers. Each book concludes with questions, possible topics for reflection or debate, and suggestions for further reading.

THE BUSHMEN (SAN) OF AFRICA

Each volume is by an acknowledged expert (international authority, fellow of a national academy, professor, or the like, together with the brightest of younger scholars and practitioners) – authors who are eager to communicate outside the too often closed realms of academe. General readers will find much to interest them, set out in straightforward but not simplistic terms. But it is above all to the eager young that the series is directed – the generation who will soon hold our precious earth and its resources and peoples in their hands and be responsible for it.

Less textbooks than sites for reflection and challenge, the series gives readers a unique route into greater awareness of our wonderful world, far and near, east and west, past and present.

Hearing Others' Voices   The series logo was created specially for us by the celebrated designer Rob Janoff, creator of the Apple logo, hopefully a feature that will play well with a young adult computer-mad audience.

The first volumes were released in November 2018, preceded by the October launching Chengdu, west China of the Chinese version of Rob Janoff's amazing personal account of how he created the famous apple logo.

****

Published so far (Spring 2022)

Birds and Humans: who are we? David Campbell Callender

Taking a bite out of the apple: a graphic designer's tale, Rob Janoff, designer

Time for the world to learn from Africa, Ruth Finnegan FBA, anthropologist, Emeritus Professor, The Open University, UK

Voices from the Christian west, Arthur Hawes, theologian, Emeritus Archdeacon, Lincoln Cathedral

From blank canvas to garment: a creative journey of discovery, Marella Campagna, fashion designer

Listen world! Evelyn Glennie, the world's premier solo percussionist.

Grass: miracle from the earth: David Campbell Callender, Irish naturalist

Native American knowledge systems, Clara Sue Kidsell, historian of science, University of North Carolina

For peace; Voices of protest and aspiration, edited by Ruth Finnegan FBA, anthropologist

Decisions, decisions, decisions, with compassion and love: voice from the headteacher's study, A headteacher

Being a poet, being an Archbishop, being human, Archbishop Rowan Williams FBA, writer, poet, theologian

Hunter-gatherers: something to learn, Alan Barnard FBA, Emeritus Professor of the Anthropology of Southern Africa, University of Edinburgh

Façonner la parole en Afrique de l'Ouest / Voices of West Africa (bilingual edition), Cecile Luguy, anthropologist

Mental health: mind, body or spirit? Voices of the other,
Venerable Arthur Hawes, theologian and mental health worker,
Emeritus Archdeacon, Lincoln Cathedral

Einstein's theory of relativity, a concise account for general readers,
H.A. Lorenz, close colleague of Einstein's

A boat refugee, a doctor, a singer – and a Lieutenant Colonel,
Dr Thao Nguyen, GP

Being a pastry cook, being a restaurant owner, and more, Stefan
Rinke, Austrian chef, Carinthia *Konditerei,* Auckland, New Zealand

An artist-priest: impossible? Rev Ernesto Lozada Uzuriaga, prize-winning Peruvian painter and British church minster

A thousand reflections on the moon, A simple view about China,
Yunxia Wu

An incredible journey, from mud hut to Cambridge,
John Shabaya, Kenyan, pastor, taxi driver

Life's journey with cartographic meanderings,
John Hunt, cartographer

Listen to this! The astounding history of quotation marks,
Ruth Finnegan, linguistic anthropologist

Will we survive? Ernest Shackleton, scientist, explorer, leader

Your amazing body, Anna, physiotherapist

Called to serve: The work of God in a crazy world,
Mike Coley, thinker

The moon, the watching witching moon,
David Campbell Callender, naturalist

Storms, the way of the mariner, Tom Schofield, sea captain

JOIN THE HEARING OTHERS' VOICES COMMUNITY

Welcome from us all, specially the series editors **Ruth** and **Roh**.

We look forward to your ideas, questions, arguments, criticisms and challenges. Let's hear your views, listen to your poems and see your poems and other materials *specially*, your photos.

It would be especially interesting to have your reactions to any of the discussion questions.

Photos and videos too, images, and links to music and poetry and thoughts please, your own and others'. The series, after all, is **Hearing Others' Voices** – yours very much included – so that's what it's all about.

https://www.facebook.com/HearingOthers/

https://www.hearingothersvoices.org/

https://balestier.com/category/hearing-others-voices/

THE BUSHMEN (SAN) OF AFRICA